THE DOCTOR TALKER

HOW SIX DETERMINED INDIVIDUALS ACCOMPLISHED THEIR DREAM OF BECOMING A DOCTOR

DR. JOHN C. TURNER

CONTRIBUTORS: DR. ANTHONY TAYLOR, DR. KHANDICIA RANDOLPH, DR. SAMARIA ROBERTS-WASHINGTON, DR. TRENTON WATSON, DR. ZAKIA GATES

John C. Turner et. al.

Enhanced DNA Publishing
www.EnhancedDNAPublishing.com
info@EnhancedDNA1.com
317-537-1438

The Doctor Talker
Copyright © 2023 Dr. John C. Turner
All rights reserved.
No portion of this publication may be reproduced, stored in any electronic system, or transmitted in any form or by any means without the written permission from the author. Brief quotations may be used in literary reviews.

ISBN-13: 979-8-9874187-9-6
Library of Congress Number: 2023916985

DEDICATION

For everyone who ever had a dream of becoming a Doctor, just know this book is evidence that your dream can become possible!

- Dr. JT

John C. Turner et. al.

TABLE OF CONTENTS

DEDICATION III
FOREWORD VII
INTRODUCTION XIII
DR. JOHN C. TURNER 19
   FROM CLASS CLOWN TO CLASS PROFESSOR 21
DR. ANTHONY K. TAYLOR 37
   PRESSURES AND PRIVILEDGES OF THE DOCTORAL JOURNEY 39
DR. KHANDICIA N. RANDOLPH 47
   RUN YOUR RACE AND NO ONE ELSE'S 49
DR. SAMARIA R. ROBERTS-WASHINGTON 69
   I AM MY SISTER AND BROTHER'S KEEPER 71
DR. TRENTON WATSON 87
   SHAKEN, BUT NOT DETERRED 89
DR. ZAKIA GATES 103
   PURSUE THE PATH TO INVITE COMMUNITY 105
INSPIRATION FOR THE NEXT GENERATION OF DOCTORS 127

FOREWORD

Celebrating the Educational Journeys of Black Doctoral Scholars

by Terrell L. Strayhorn, PhD

In the realm of education, there is a profound need for diverse voices and perspectives to be acknowledged, elevated, and embraced. Throughout history, countless individuals from underrepresented, underserved, and misrepresented communities have faced significant obstacles along their educational journeys, often encountering systemic barriers that have hindered their progress and success. Among the many system-impacted groups in higher education, Black students seeking doctoral degrees face particularly sizable challenges.

Black doctoral student challenges vary in scope. For example, reams of research show that these challenges include limited access to funding and professional resources, lack of role models and support networks, as well as pervasive racial biases and 'stereotype threat,' to name a few. Despite these obstacles, their resilience, determination, grit, and optimism fuel Black doctoral students' path through academia in ways that bring 'Black excellence' to life.

It is with great pleasure that I introduce this exciting new book, which chronicles six remarkable life stories and educational journeys of Black doctoral students who have defied the odds and successfully achieved their dreams of earning a doctorate. Their captivating narratives reveal the incredible strength, unwavering optimism, and upbeat determination required for many students of color, expressly African Americans, to overcome the significant barriers and disparities that exist within the realm of higher education today.

Current statistics underscore the imperative need for increasing representation of Black doctoral degree holders in the United States. According to the National Center for Education Statistics, only 5.4% of doctoral degrees awarded were earned by Black students (NCES, 2019). This disproportionately low representation within the echelons of academia not only perpetuates a lack of diversity but also limits our collective capacity to address contemporary social, economic, and scientific challenges that require a diverse range of cross-disciplinary perspectives.

This book provides a platform for amplifying the untold stories and unsung accomplishments of these extraordinary individuals. By sharing the experiences of these Black students who defied the odds and have gone on to achieve doctoral success, the volume aims to inspire and motivate others who may face similar challenges. It is through these stories that the book holds promise for catalyzing important conversations about the urgent need for change in higher education and the pressing necessity to create a far more inclusive academic environment.

Each chapter of this book delves into the unique journey of one of these remarkable individuals, illuminating the challenges they faced, the sacrifices they made, and the triumphs they achieved. Some encountered financial hardships, navigating the complex world of student loans, part- and full-time work, internships, and, yes, the reality of struggling to find adequate sources of funding. Others lay it all bare - detailing how they dealt with isolation, grappled with the sense of being "the only one" in classrooms, research labs, and academic spaces. Balancing the demands of their doctoral studies with unrelenting personal responsibilities and, at times, societal expectations based on race, gender, and their intersections, these individuals demonstrated remarkable resilience, respect, and resolve in the face of adversity.

Their stories also reveal the transformative power of mentorship and support in shaping successful academic trajectories, especially for Black doctoral students. Whether through the guidance of a supportive advisor, the inspiration of a peer, the work of a distant scholar of color, or the encouragement of family and friends, authors of each autobiographical chapter found solace and guidance *internally* and *externally* that propelled them forward when the journey seemed insurmountable.

The narratives within these pages represent not only the individual triumphs of Black doctoral students who found a way or made one, but they also serve as a call to action for educational institutions, campus leaders, policymakers, and society at large. The time is now, and we are the ones we've been waiting for. We must recognize the immense value that diversity brings to the table and actively work towards dismantling the barriers that limit full access, participation, and success of Black students in higher education, especially within doctoral education.

Actively working toward dismantling obstacles that limit the full participation and success of Black students in doctoral education requires a multi-faceted approach. Institutions must prioritize diversity, equity, and inclusion by proactively recruiting and retaining Black doctoral students through well-designed, targeted outreach programs, bridge services, and scholarships. Additionally, creating mentoring programs that intentionally connect Black students with doctoral faculty who can provide career advice, research guidance, and out-of-classroom support is essential. Furthermore, implementing anti-bias, anti-racist training for faculty and staff can help address systemic problems within academia and initiate long-overdue curricular revision for some programs. In terms of finances, increasing funding opportunities, loan forgiveness benefits, and reducing overall costs of doctoral education can significantly alleviate economic burdens borne by Black doctoral students and their families.

Indeed, this book serves as an invaluable resource for aspiring Black students themselves who may be considering pursuing a doctoral degree. It provides a blueprint for navigating the challenges, cultivating resilience, and seeking out the resources necessary for success.

It's an upfront, honest peek behind the curtains, so to speak, that exposes the dreams, aspirations, and harsh realities associated with pursuing a doctoral degree—what some have come to call *studying while Black* (SWB). By showcasing these first-hand accounts of SWB, the book aims to foster a sense of community and solidarity among

Black students pursuing academia and reassure them that they are not alone in their journey. That they matter. They're enough. And, contrary to popular belief, they belong there.

In bearing witness to the remarkable achievements and transformative journeys of these six Black doctoral students, the book seems to ignite passion, inspire change, and urge a more inclusive academic ecosystem. Let their stories serve as a testament to the immeasurable potential that lies within everyone, regardless of their background, race, origin, or circumstances. Together, let us celebrate their accomplishments and strive for a future where every individual has an equal and equitable opportunity to achieve their dreams.

Keep shining,

Terrell L. Strayhorn, Ph.D.
Professor of Education and Psychology
Director, Center for the Study of HBCUs
Principal Investigator, The Belonging Lab
Virginia Union University

INTRODUCTION

Too many conversations have started like this for many Doctorate degree earners...

"So, what is your name?"

"I am Doctor ...."

"Oh, so you're a Doctor, what hospital do you work at?"

"I'm not a medical Doctor."

"Oh, so you're a professor, what school do you teach at?"

"I'm not that kind of Doctor either..."

"Oh... so what kind of Doctor are you?"

For Doctors that have dealt with this frustrating conversation, I feel for you. With over 50+ different types of Doctorate degrees and hundreds of Doctorate granting Institutions, it can be exhausting to have to explain what type of Doctor you are to every person that is interested in knowing what kind of Doctor you actually are. What makes things even more frustrating can be the fact that when you have a Doctorate degree from a Higher Education institution that is either a for-profit, online, or non-brick and mortar location, it now really makes people question the legitimacy of your Doctorate degree even more. The common preconceived notion is that the only real Doctorate degrees constitute either Medical Doctors and their specializations or PhDs. But now with so many different regionally and nationally accredited higher education institutions offering Doctorate degrees other than MDs and PhDs, along with BIPOC and individuals from underserved populations are completing Doctorates at a very high level, it is crucial that awareness is spread of the fact that these Doctorate degrees are earned through hard work and that they all deserve to be celebrated. You are not Dr. Dre, Dr. Pepper, or Dr. Seuss. You are a real Doctor who earned your Doctorate degree at an accredited institution, and you should be recognized and celebrated for your achievement.

We must realize that not all Doctorate degree completion levels are created equal, but the rigor of completing a Doctorate degree always requires much work, persistence, and tenacity to get to the Doctorate finish line. While an individual may have to complete their Doctorate degree at an institution that might be for-profit, religious, online, or non-brick and mortar, many of these individuals have had little to no choice to do so. Many non-profit, PWIs, and Very High/High Research Carnegie classified institutions have historically and regularly excluded BIPOC and individuals from underserved populations from pursuing Doctorate degrees. This systematic and discriminatory exclusion has led many of them to have to pursue their Doctorate degree elsewhere, as many of those aforementioned institutions still hold quotas on how many BIPOC and underserved individuals that they allow to pursue their Doctorate programs during each admission cycle. Also, many less popular Doctorate degree offering institutions provide better funding opportunities through professional development, scholarships, and tuition reimbursement employer agreements that allow prospective Doctorate degree students to fund a Doctorate degree partially or even in full. Unfortunately, the most well-known Doctorate degree offering institutions often have very few to no funding opportunities, which can leave Doctorate students in huge amounts of debt, and many run out of funding before they can even complete their Doctorate degree. No one has the right to downplay where someone has earned their doctorate and the major in which they earned their Doctorate degree. Each individual makes the best decision for their time, money, and peace of mind to complete Doctorate degrees which will help them excel their careers, passions, and futures. They should be celebrated for their achievement as entering the Academy of which only 2% of the people in the world complete a Doctorate degree and an even very smaller percentage of individuals complete the accomplishment as BIPOC or from underserved populations is incredible. We all need to celebrate with that individual together.

So, when you see a new Doctor who has completed their Doctorate degree, please do not question, or belittle their credentials. The late nights of reading, the months of researching and studying, the hours of writing; all that effort to earn the Doctorate degree which that individual did should not be taken for granted. The individual is now a

Doctor and may end up doing more beneficial things for society than the individuals who got their Doctorate degree from well-known institutions. To the individuals who have a Doctor of Pharmacy, Doctor of Education, Doctor of Ministry, Doctor of Social Work, Doctor of Business Administration, Doctor of Strategic Leadership, Doctor of Behavioral Health, Doctor of Organizational Leadership, Doctor of Psychology, Doctor of Public Health, Doctor of Dentistry, and all the other Doctors… Your Doctorate degree matters! It is truly an incredible achievement to complete a Doctorate degree! No matter where the institution they completed their Doctorate degree, they deserve to get the love, support, and distinct honor of being called "Doctor".

So how did this vision of a book dedicated towards the success of Doctorate degree completers come about? Well, look no further than a LinkedIn post in March 2023 that the Lead Author on *The Doctor Talker* book Dr. John C. Turner posted a simple question at the beginning which stated "So you want to become a DOCTOR?" After posting this post with 9 tips on steps for prospective Doctorate degree seekers to follow if they were interested in becoming a Doctor, the post went viral. With nearly 460,000 impressions, 8,500 reactions, 800 comments, and 400 reposts, the conversation on how to become a Doctor was born. So after, a conversation inviting defended and conferred Doctorate degree earners started to commence on LinkedIn Live and YouTube called "The Doc Chat" Show. On this show, Doctors from all kinds of Doctorate degree academic backgrounds came together to share their doctoral journeys. In just five months time, "The Doc Chat " show brought on nearly 50 different Doctors to talk about their doctoral journeys to becoming Doctors, and registered nearly 25,000 views combined on the LinkedIn and YouTube websites. Now, the doctoral journey stories continue to be shared in this amazing book "The Doctor Talker".

The following chapters are personal life and Doctoral journeys from six Doctors who earned their Doctorate degrees in different academic majors. We hope that by sharing these stories and tips, along with sharing the truth of how these Doctorate degrees made a difference in our lives and careers, that future students are encouraged to pursue this level of education. Whatever your passions might be, there is a Doctorate out there that you can achieve. Just know that the Doctorate Degree that you earned does matter!

DR. JOHN C. TURNER

Dr. John C. Turner, Ph.D. aka The Professor JT, a native of Indianapolis, Indiana, is an alumnus of Indiana State University where he received his B.S. in Electronics Technology and M.S. in Student Affairs & Higher Education. Dr. Turner successfully completed a Ph.D. in Urban Education Studies from the Indiana University School of Education at Indiana University Indianapolis. Dr. Turner's academic research focus investigates the retention and success of the minority males & BIPOC K-Doctorate students, staff, and faculty. Dr. Turner is the CEO and Owner of The Professor JT Educational Counseling LLC. Dr. Turner has been a Conference Speaker, Model, Community Panelist, and Keynote Speaker, along with being an Education Advocate who creates community, school, organization, corporation, networking, and programming opportunities to discuss societal, systemic, & DEIB issues. Dr. Turner is host of "The Doc Chat" Show on LinkedIn and YouTube which highlights the doctoral journeys of Doctors from all kinds of Doctorate degree majors. Dr. Turner is a member of Kappa Alpha Psi Fraternity, Inc.

FROM CLASS CLOWN TO CLASS PROFESSOR

"The function of education is to teach one to think intensively, and to think critically. Intelligence plus character - that is the goal of true education."

- Dr. Martin Luther King, Jr.

Introduction

Every Doctor has a journey, and every journey begins with a calling. I remember exactly where I heard mine, somewhere completely unexpected. It was in the middle of my senior year band class. Something my band teacher said that period would stick with me throughout my life and higher education. To this day, I don't know how we got onto the topic of Doctorate degrees, but I can remember him clearly stating, "you can get a Doctorate degree in ANYTHING!" That small message opened my eyes to what could be possible for me. Though I knew the path of my life was not leading me into medical practice, I was suddenly certain that somehow, Dr. John C. Turner was the name I was going to have one day. I was convinced that a Doctorate degree was going to be in my future.

Life before the Doctorate Program

When I was a young boy in grade school, my mother used to take my younger brother and me along to her college classes. She was enrolled at Marian College in Indianapolis, Indiana with a dream of becoming a teacher. I remember my brother and I sitting for hours in those classrooms, libraries, and auditoriums as our mother wrote and studied for her lessons. My brother and I, being two young Black boys from inner-city Indianapolis, did not see Marian College as anything but a place that kept us away from our friends at home. We wanted so badly to be playing outside with the rest of the kids our age, and instead, we were stuck at a boring campus. While we would rather be anywhere else at the time, little did we know our first-hand witnessing of our mother's educational journey would have a great impact on our lives.

In grade school, I was always a class clown, trying to be the center of attention. You could often find me missing recess and getting into trouble for wanting to speak out and be heard. All I wanted was to laugh and have fun with my brother and friends. Learning, on the other hand, was not something I enjoyed very much. But seeing our mother cramming for classes and putting in so much effort to succeed in her program was putting something into our spirits that was deeper than we could have ever predicted. Even though I was still a boy, I remember how moving it was for me to see my mother walk across the graduation stage to get her bachelor's degree in Elementary education. All those years of hard work and dragging us rowdy boys to all those classes finally paid off for my mother. After a summer of job hunting while simultaneously preparing us boys for another academic year on top of finalizing a divorce with my stepfather, my mother got offered the opportunity to teach at the same inner-city school my brother was attending. She was finally getting her chance to fulfill her dream of becoming a classroom teacher. Tragically, she never came to see that dream come to pass. Only one day before my mother was supposed to start her dream job teaching at an elementary school, my best friend found her lying in our driveway. She had just worked overnight the last two nights at her job and had barely slept in the last 48 hours. After dropping my brother off at his football game, she went home to mow the lawn. When she finished the task, she collapsed from a mild heart attack at the age of 40 years old. Though she never got to see her dream come to fruition of teaching in the classroom, she succeeded at instilling a love of education and a drive to pursue becoming an educator in my own heart. Though my own journey to teaching in an academic field would have its turns and difficulties, my mother inspired something deep in my soul when I grew up seeing her commitments firsthand. She may not have had the chance to teach but by example, she led me to become the educator I am today.

After the passing of my mother, I struggled greatly through all of high school. My academics suffered as I was in a college preparatory catholic high school that felt leaps and bounds ahead of my intelligence level. I had to take summer school at a neighborhood public school to make up for two failing grades that I had my freshman year. The only class I was excelling in was band. Those "A" grades are what kept my GPA above 2.0 as I was a "C" average student throughout the rest of my curriculum. By the time I graduated high school, I had a 2.2 GPA, which was just enough to qualify for financial aid at a college or university. However, it was still going to be difficult with a GPA that low for me to get accepted at a four-year college program. I never could have done it if not for a Black male admissions officer from Indiana State University, who was seeking out Black students who had completed an inner-city Indianapolis non-profit program at the Center for Leadership Development called Self Discovery. I got involved in the program because it helped prepare Black and Brown students in the Indianapolis area for college life. So that following year I started out at Indiana State. I was an undecided student on an academic plan where I had to meet with an advisor every Monday to review my class work throughout that semester. I couldn't stand going to those sessions. I did not want to have to see this guy every week to go over my grades and the only way out of it was to get the grades up. So that first semester... I smashed it! Putting in the extra effort, I got my GPA up to 3.3, and on top of that, I gained the confidence that I could improve my academic performance further. That one successful semester in college propelled my educational journey forward and would reshape it for good.

I made the decision midway through my sophomore year to major in Electronics Technology. I thought this would lead me to a career creating video games, which I loved playing as a kid. Come to find out, this work was more blue-collar. The major's purpose was to give knowledge to students to work in careers with electrical components, PLCs, lighting, and other forms of electrical technologies. I stuck with the major because I was learning a lot about computer programs, I enjoyed it and did well in the classes. Unfortunately, starting off as an undecided student for a year and a half pushed my financial aid to run out, as I still had an entire year of coursework to complete for my bachelor's degree. I didn't have money to spare for classes or my room and board. I was anxious about the thought of having to balance my schoolwork with a job and an apartment for the first time until God delivered a miracle.

A Resident Assistant position opened on campus the summer before my fifth year of college, and I was hired for the role. I didn't know the first thing about being a Resident Assistant other than they got their room and board paid for along with some of their tuition. But that was what I needed to finish college, so I took up the position of Resident Assistant on a Freshman Resident Hall floor with 33 of the rowdiest young men I would ever come to meet. What I thought was just going to be a year-long, one-and-done deal of Residence Hall life, turned into something I never would have imagined. I really loved working with these male students, and in turn, I applied to the Student Affairs and Higher Education master's program at Indiana State University. I became an Assistant Hall Director for both years of my master's program, and I received two more years of room & board, with tuition and a work stipend. I went from taking a job out of desperation to falling right into a career field of education that my mother had dropped in my spirit all those years ago.

Life during the Doctorate Program

My education career came to an abrupt stop after one year as a Residence Hall Director. I ended up moving back to Indianapolis and what I thought was a straight path to getting a job in Higher Education and obtaining my master's degree, ran right into the sad occurrence of a recession that made getting a job extremely difficult. But once again what I thought was a hiccup, ended up being exactly what I needed to get back to working in the field of Higher Education. During the recession, I took a job working in the Men's department of JC Penney. I remember running into a former friend of mine who graduated with the same Electronics Technology degree from ISU. Upon seeing me working in the men's section he shouted, "John Turner, what are YOU DOING HERE?" I knew he had a great job at the time, while I was making roughly 9 dollars an hour as a customer service associate.

I kept pushing through that role for a year until an Assistant Manager job opened at The Sherwin-Williams Paint Company. Don't worry, this ties into the story too. I took that job, not even knowing anything about paint. I remember being introduced to flat paint, a term used to refer to paint with a matte texture that dries quickly, and my response was "What is FLAT about it?" I had no awareness they were talking about the sheen and not the actual figurativeness of the paint product. I learned so much in that Assistant Manager role, but something that stuck with me deeply is when I would drive past Ivy Tech Community College on my way to work every day. As I saw the campus pass by, I would say "In Jesus' Name, I am going to work there." I still had the passion to work with college students and knew that I wanted to be back at a higher education institution as an educator. After a year and a half, an opportunity came about for an Assistant Director of Academic Advising at Ivy Tech Community College. What made this role even more special was that it was an Advisor role working as a liaison with the School of Business. So, for me, between moving back to Indianapolis, the recession starting, and leading me to work at JC Penney (a corporate business), and then at The Sherwin Williams Paint Company (a corporate business), I was more prepared than I possibly could have been before to receive a job back in education as an Academic Advisor connecting students with business classes, majors, and careers.

I felt an instantaneous connection at Ivy Tech Community College and the students, and I started to receive opportunities outside of my Academic Advising job. A colleague working in the Academic Advising department taught sections of the IVYT Student Success courses on campus and suggested that I do the same as an adjunct professor. Not only was it great extra income, but it allowed me to explore another area of higher education as a faculty affairs member when most of my experience had been on the student affairs side. After teaching my first traditional course class, I was brought into a meeting with another Black male educator and our White female IVYT courses department director. They both had an idea of creating an affinity section of the IVYT course that was specifically for Black males. Research has shown us that Black males had the lowest retention and completion rates of the IVYT course, and it was brought up as an idea that the two of us Black male faculty members teach a section of the course each to help combat these numbers. In the end, after one semester of teaching these two classes, the completion rate went from 25% in the traditional IVYT courses, to 65% of the Black males completing these two courses. Over the next few years, similar sections of this IVYT Black male affinity course would be taught with similar progress in retention and completion results. I was finding my calling again in higher education and I was loving every moment of it.

Eventually, Ivy Tech Community College was approached by Indiana University School of Education in Indianapolis about recruiting students into their just recently formed Urban Education Studies (UES) PhD program. Not only was the opportunity open for Ivy Tech Community College employees, but Ivy Tech Community College would pay for up to 6 credit hours every semester towards the completion of the Doctorate Degree. After the last season of thriving in higher education again, I looked on it as the opportunity of a lifetime. I could pursue a Doctorate degree in a program I had come to find myself enjoying and passionate about. I never would have predicted I would find myself in this position, and it took me all the way back to my high school band teacher saying, "You can get a Doctorate degree in ANYTHING!" I spoke to the program chair of the UES program before I applied and expressed my interest in doing a dissertation about the work, we were doing at Ivy Tech Community College with the Black Male Affinity Course. He gave me insights about applying and the encouragement that he would love to see my application towards next year's cohort. I began to gather my application materials and recommendation letters, and by December of that year, I had everything I needed in Indiana University's Graduate School Admission office for the UES Doctorate program. I could not believe this young Black male who graduated high school with a 2.2 GPA was applying to a PhD program.

I interviewed alongside 20 other individuals who had an interest in getting into the Ph.D. program that next February. My interviewers loved that I came well-prepared with my possible dissertation topic in mind and clear post-doctorate career goals. After a mere two weeks, I received the news that I had gotten into the PhD program. Upon reading the congratulatory email at noon while in my cubicle at work, I immediately went to my car and cried tears of joy that I had made it. Over the next few months, I would start to put the pieces in place to prepare for my August enrollment as a Ph.D. Doctorate student at Indiana University. I can hardly accurately describe the elation I felt upon acceptance, the excitement of pursuing a Doctorate degree, and the relief at having the chance to do it basically for free in my hometown of Indianapolis, Indiana. I wept joyful tears because a dream was coming true, and I knew my mother would be proud.

Even though that first semester of the Urban Education Studies PhD program was eye-opening from a knowledge and learning standpoint, the bigger revelation for me was the writing and rigor of it all, and it really felt like I wasn't prepared. The program was set up as a cohort, and there were 10 of us total, 8 Women and 2 Males. I was the only Black male in the cohort. I thought I was a great writer because I had years of experience writing blogs and papers before I started the PhD program. I knew I was capable to sit and write quickly for long periods of time with no problem producing a great final product. But there are levels to writing academically that I, and many other Black Doctorate students, are not prepared for in ways that put us at a disadvantage in these programs. I struggled mightily in my first qualitative methodologies studies course with the concept of writing in APA. This hadn't been the standard in the academic courses I had taken previously. Learning about theories and methodologies, conducting literature reviews, and comprehending so many dense pieces while trying to put together academic papers made me question if I was even capable of writing at this intense level. I barely made it out of that first qualitative methodologies studies course with a passing grade. I remember crying as I received a 14/20 on my last course exam which got me a course final grade of a "B-".

Seeing the long road ahead, I knew had to learn how to take care of my mind, body, and soul to make it through the years of coursework the PhD program requires. I was working full-time, being a full-time Doctorate student, and being active in my community and social life. To do all this and still attend city events, family and friend's functions, and take care of my own home, I had to figure out how I would take care of myself too. I made an intentional commitment to take Sundays off, completely. I did not do any school or full-time work on Sundays, as I dedicated that day to going to church, resting, and preparing for the week to come. The weekdays were long as I would work from 8 AM – 5 PM and then drive over to the PhD campus for classes 2 or 3 days out of the week for 6 PM – 9 PM classes. I found that affording myself a full day of rest was not a sacrifice of my time, but crucial to my success during all the other days that required my full energy and attention. Speaking of attention, I couldn't really afford any for my dating life during the PhD program. When I would try, I really struggled with success in that area. I started to think that Ph.D. also meant "Pretty Horrible Dating". But I did what I needed to do to stay focused on my goal, and today I'm thankful I focused my energy where it was needed and kept myself healthy. One of the best things I was able to do since I had an idea of the dissertation research was start collecting research and writing papers for my PhD courses along that dissertation research direction. It allowed me to complete my coursework with already having a literature review and much of the first three chapters of my dissertation already completed. I would knock out defending my qualifying exams and dissertation proposal within 3 months of each other and could start to see the finish line of my PhD Doctorate degree. Well… so I thought…

Life of Completing the Doctorate Degree & Life now as a Doctor

The week after I defended my dissertation proposal, I was facing down another personal tragedy. My father passed away after dealing with years of different illnesses. He had struggled with substance abuse throughout his life, and his passing hit me hard as he was my only living parent. I wanted to get through with my Doctorate degree for him to see me get hooded. He had made it to my other two college graduations, and I couldn't fathom him not attending this one. But I knew more than ever that I had to complete my Doctorate degree. My parents were with me in spirit, and I wanted to make them proud. I investigated creating a qualitative study, my research data collection method was conducting interviews of 5 Black male students who I was able to track down after several years of being in the IVYT Black male first-year experience affinity course. The interviews were powerful, these students provided their thoughts and recollections of how their lives were before, during, and after they took the course with me as their instructor. Tears were shed and laughs were shared, and each student shook my hand and said thank you after the interviews were over. It was a relief for these students to share their hearts with me on how much our college class had shaped the trajectory of their lives. Using William Cross' Black Identity Development Theory as my theoretical framework, I was able to start to put together the first three chapters of the first draft of my dissertation and send it to the dissertation chair. I felt elated that I had put together such an incredible body of work at such a traumatic time in my life. I had no clue that the next year and a half would be the real test on the path to my Doctorate degree completion.

As I waited for a response from my dissertation chair about the status of my dissertation, I started to prepare for graduation. I ordered my cap and gown, got a custom stole, and started to let people know that Dr. John C. Turner was on his way toward graduation at the end of the Spring semester. My dissertation chair had set a date at the end of March for me to defend my dissertation and my graduation would be that next May. As the beginning of March came, I remember sitting in my office at my new job, with my dissertation defense scheduled three weeks away, and saying to myself, "As long as the World does not fall apart in these next 3 weeks, I will get to my dissertation defense." I had no clue that those words would mean so much with what transpired those next 3 weeks. In the second week of March, there were reports of a virus that was making its way around the World. COVID-19 started to wreak havoc on the lives of everyone in the United States. By the end of that second week of March, the country was starting to shut down. As I started to roll into the third week of March, my dissertation chair shared the most dreaded news that no doctoral candidate wants to hear… "We are going to have to postpone your dissertation defense as your dissertation has an extensive number of errors that need to be rectified before defending your work." Not only was the World shutting down, but my dissertation defense had gotten shut down as well. I was devastated. I got connected with a member of my dissertation committee who ended up helping me with getting my dissertation to the level it needed to be defended.

With COVID-19 raging on, I was now working from home and eventually decided to resign from my role at the Center for Leadership Development to concentrate on completing my Doctorate degree. The back and forth with my dissertation committee member was a tedious experience, as I would get my edits sent back their way in 1-2 days but would then have to wait 1-2 weeks for them to get a response back on my work. As the summer trudged on, I would sit for hours, from 8 AM – 3 PM just writing. I would only get up to use the bathroom or grab a quick bite to eat. As this process lasted into the fall, I started to get concerned that completing my Ph.D. was never going to happen. Finally, the dissertation committee member I worked with was contacted by my dissertation committee chair to see about my progress around the first week of September. They evaluated my dissertation and let me know that it was nearly ready for defense. I made some final edits, and the committee chair advised me that I should have an editor go over the entire body of work to fix grammar mistakes and APA format. He suggested a Professor from the University of Iowa to conduct my edits, but it was not cheap. I ended up paying over 700 dollars to get my dissertation edited. But when I resubmitted the edited dissertation, I was given the final go-ahead to set my defense date. I was elated that what seemed to be delayed and possibly destroyed was not denied.

I waited eight months to reach my dissertation defense date. At the time, everyone was still following COVID-19 distancing protocols, and my dissertation defense was conducted through Zoom. However, because of this I was able to have friends, colleagues, and family from all over the country view my dissertation defense live. I even had the opportunity for my journey to come full circle, as I could defend my dissertation from the campus of Ivy Tech Community College, the same place I taught my first IVYT Black male affinity section course. I was passionate about my research, and it meant the world to me to be able to defend my dissertation on the thoughts and words of the Black male students that I taught, right in my hometown of Indianapolis.

I felt prepared, dressed exceptionally well, and opened my dissertation defense with a quick prayer. This was how I got into the "zone" and felt ready to accomplish. I breezed through the presentation portion of my defense, hitting every point with precision and exactness with the research I knew from top to bottom. Then came the cross-examination from the committee, and they laid right into me with every single question. There were moments I felt rattled as the questions started to question my research decisions and why went in the direction I did to complete my dissertation. But I kept my composure and answered every question as thoroughly as I could to my best ability, with transparency, assurance, and making sure each question was answered in full. After a half hour of cross-examination, the dissertation committee went into a separate Zoom room to deliberate on my defense. I took the time to thank all my friends and family who showed up to support me. This simple act of showing gratitude to each person one at a time calmed my nerves as I waited for my dissertation committee to return. Finally, after almost 20 minutes, the dissertation committee returned to make their announcement. They had decided that I had passed my dissertation defense with some minor errors in need of revisions. I cried a big ugly cry as I thanked my dissertation committee members and all my attendees. I unbuttoned my dress shirt to reveal a custom t-shirt I had made, that announced myself finally as John Cleo Turner, PhD. I became the first Ivy Tech Community College employee to graduate with an Urban Education Studies Ph.D. from Indiana University School of Education in Indianapolis. Today, I continue to work in Education, inspiring undergraduates to become the next generation of Doctors. It is clear to me that my help always and continues to come from the Lord Jesus Christ. He led me on a journey that at times I believed was not possible, but despite all my doubts, I was able to answer the call on my heart to become a Doctor.

DR. ANTHONY K. TAYLOR

Dr. Anthony K. Taylor, was born and raised in Chicago, IL. The youngest of four siblings and passionate about healthcare and helping others find solutions to their unmet medical needs. Dr. Taylor completed his education at A.T. Still University with a doctorate degree in health sciences and a concentration in organizational leadership. He is married to his husband of 8 years and has two very intelligent and handsome sons. He is a member of the American College of Healthcare Executives and Kappa Alpha Psi fraternity. Dr. Taylor has worked in the pharmaceutical and healthcare industry for 18 years and has held positions of increasing responsibility.

PRESSURES AND PRIVILEDGES OF THE DOCTORAL JOURNEY

"Education is the most powerful weapon which you can use to change the world."

- Nelson Mandela

Introduction

For as long as I can remember I have been influenced by strong leaders who taught me that I could make a difference in someone else's life. This passion to lead others was initiated by my father who was the eldest of seven siblings, a military veteran, and leader within our local community. Unfortunately, he died at the age of 68 due to complications with congestive heart failure and kidney disease. He was the patriarch within our family. He was also a leader within the company in which he worked for over 25 years. By watching him I learned how to actively listen, to learn from my mistakes, to be accountable, and to strive to become an effective leader within my own endeavors.

My mother was the matriarch within our family and an active community member who always advocated for positive change. She was the first in our family to pursue a career in healthcare which served as the catalyst for me and my siblings. She taught me to never settle, to be selfless, and to always lead by example. Unfortunately, my mother passed away from a sudden heart attack in 2021, two years before I would graduate with my doctoral degree. However, I know that my mom and dad are with me throughout my journey in life and they continue to inspire me. There have been other leaders who have influenced me to go above and beyond in my career and my life. Some honorable mentions include my family, colleagues, former professors, and other organizational leaders.

When I was about 10 years old, a family member asked me what I wanted to be when I grew up. I immediately responded that I wanted to be a doctor. I then proceeded to tell them that I wanted to be the first black CEO of a hospital in Chicago, where I was born and raised. I felt extremely confident and capable because of the lessons my parents taught me. As a child, I had no idea that there were different types of doctors and I also thought that all doctors worked in hospitals. As an adult, I learned about the different types of doctors, including but not limited to Doctor of Health Sciences (DHSc), Doctor of Philosophy (Ph.D.), Doctor of Medicine (M.D.), Doctor of Education (Ed.D.), Juris Doctor or a Doctor of Jurisprudence (JD), Doctor of Pharmacy (PharmD), Doctor of Business Administration (DBA), Doctor of Healthcare Administration (DHA), Doctor of Social Work (DSW), Doctor of Nursing Practice (DNP), Doctor of Public Health (DrPH), Doctor of Ministry

(D.Min.), Doctor of Psychology (Psy.D.), Doctor of Chiropractic (D.C.) and the list goes on.

Hence, my vision shifted ever so slightly over time. I am now a Doctor of Health Sciences and throughout my career I have observed that African Americans and other minorities are underrepresented within the field of clinical research and pharmaceutical leadership. I want to lead a pharmaceutical or healthcare organization to ensure that underserved patients have access to life-saving medication and to address the fact that representation matters.

At one point in my life, a doctorate degree felt unattainable. When I was 23 years old I got married and I became a father one year after that. I felt an immediate sense of joy and responsibility to protect and provide. Seven years later my youngest son was born, and those same feelings of joy mixed with anxiousness reemerged. I am now remarried to my husband of 8 years and am grateful to have married my best friend. I have finally achieved my goal of becoming a doctor. I no longer feel that a doctorate degree is beyond reach but instead know that all things are possible if you have faith. My focus then was to work, gain experience, build my resume, and establish a stable career in clinical research within the pharmaceutical industry.

Life before the Doctorate Program

I worked and went to school intermittently for a total of eighteen years. At times I struggled to afford putting myself through school and providing for my family. Before venturing into the doctoral journey, I obtained master's degrees in business and project management, bioethics, and pharmacy. My career began as a pharmacy technician at a major retail pharmacy. Prior to that, I wanted to learn about all aspects of the healthcare industry to evaluate which direction I wanted to pursue. I worked as a volunteer in a physical therapy clinic, as an office assistant at a community health not-for-profit organization, and as a senior medic in the U.S. Army.

In the Army, I learned about emergency medical treatment, triaging to determine patients' urgent needs and a leader's role in navigating teams through unfamiliar circumstances. The military taught me to always be ready for the unexpected, calm in the face of adversity, and advocate for justice and equality for others.

Throughout my career, I focused on leading and voicing to ensure that diverse patient populations are represented in clinical research studies. As a healthcare leader in the field of clinical research, it is critical to understand and ascertain the patient's perspective through patient-reported outcomes. Through personal and professional experience, I have observed the need for representation from African Americans and others on issues involving diversity in organizational leadership and opportunities in health care that benefit the whole person, and not only the disease or therapeutic need.

Furthering my education was key to success. It was the fuel to the engine. I knew that having a doctorate degree was something that no one could ever take away from me and could be used to advance the prospects of underrepresented groups within the healthcare community. It took me a while to find the right educational institution and degree program where I felt like a part of the university and that my input was valued. I researched and applied to A.T. Still University. I applied in whole person healthcare and founders of osteopathic medicine. After speaking with the recruiter, I was enthralled by what the college had to offer.

My aim was to start the doctoral program focusing on the voice of underrepresented patient populations and finish the program having elevated the need for diversity, equity, and inclusion within healthcare leadership, policy, and practice.

Life during the Doctorate Program

I vividly recall starting my first week of the doctoral program and wanting to journalize every experience so that I wouldn't forget how that moment impacted my life. Below is the first journal entry I wrote in the pursuit of the doctoral degree:

Tomorrow, Monday 23 March 2020 marks the first day of my doctoral pursuit! I am nervous and excited, I guess you can say anxious. Let the journey begin...

There were many more journal entries throughout the course of the 3-year journey of my doctoral pursuit. Several major events occurred during this time including the Covid-19 pandemic and lockdown in March 2020, just two weeks before I started school. My mother subsequently passed away on July 2nd, 2021, and there was a heightened sense of awareness for diversity, equity, inclusion, and justice as the murder of George Floyd was broadcast live on TV around the world.

This heinous crime and injustice were the impetus that necessitated discussions for equality in every facet of human life including our work environments, schools, healthcare systems, politics, and courtrooms. There is a tremendous need for more African-American scientists to be seen as leaders and representatives in the pharmaceutical and healthcare industry.

My motivation for pursuing a doctoral degree was to ensure that the patient's voice is always heard in clinical research settings and to use the attained knowledge and skills to be a positive influence and change agent for patients. I firmly stand behind the belief that "experience is the best teacher." Most aspects of life can be taught, but to fully understand where a patient is coming from, you must listen to their experiences, collaborate with them to identify viable solutions and empathize where you can. This will enable scientist-leaders to develop better practices and clinical studies with the patient being top of mind. In keeping with the journal writing, I wrote this entry mid-way through my program:

Today, Wednesday 30 March 2022 marks two years since I started the DHSC program in pursuit of my doctorate. It has been a tumultuous ride since losing my mom in July 2021 and getting married on 31 Jan 2022, but somehow, I'm surviving. It is a struggle to balance family, work, and school but GOD is making it all possible.

Completing the Doctorate Degree and Life as a Doctor

Change of any kind does not come easy. It takes reinforcement of behaviors and perseverance to implement change. Pursuing a doctoral degree means having the ability to accept that things must change. Some of these changes may include learning to prioritize personal responsibilities like family obligations against homework assignments and manuscript deadlines. As most graduate students come to understand, pursuing a doctorate degree is not for the faint at heart, meaning you must be self-motivated and willing to accept constructive criticism.

During my doctoral pursuit, I had to learn and practice how to write as a scholar to effectively present an argument for and against the issue at hand. There were times when I felt discouraged from staying up late into the evening to turn in my assignments, only to receive an unfavorable grade or harsh feedback. However, constructive criticism helped me to sharpen my critical thinking skills, evaluate fact from fiction, and distinguish evidence from emotion. In class, I often challenged myself to provide complete responses to discussion questions and to learn about different experiences from my classmates and professors.

Three years felt like forever for me at times, especially when balancing school with family and work obligations.

Whenever I felt like giving up, I would remember hearing this mantra "Once a task has begun, never rest until it's done, be the labor large or small, do it well or not at all". Now I am officially a doctor with all the rights, privileges, and responsibilities bestowed upon me pertaining thereto. I have also made some life-long friendships with classmates, faculty, and staff during the journey which will always be cherished as they too helped me arrive at the destination.

DR. KHANDICIA N. RANDOLPH

A native of the Southside of Chicago and the oldest of eight, author Dr. Khandicia N. Randolph obtained her Bachelor of Arts degree from the University of Missouri and holds a degree in Master of Public Administration with a specialization in Public Policy, a degree in Master of Arts in Law from Regent University's School of Law, and her Doctor of Strategic Leadership degree from Regent University, School of Business and Leadership. Dr. Randolph presents domestically and internationally on topics such as effective communication and leadership development and is a published author in textbooks and academic journals and a prolific speaker. Her research interests include leadership and organizational development and theoretical constructs, especially the mitigating effects of race and culture. Pursuing her passion for leadership development and organizational development and effectiveness, the author yearns to help nonprofit organizations function optimally. Dr. Randolph is the owner of Finer Consulting Services, a leadership and organizational development and effectiveness firm. She is the author of the book *The Black American Church: Leadership Dispensation and Challenges*. In her spare time, Dr. Randolph enjoys traveling internationally, shopping, and spending time with her family and friends. Dr. Randolph is a Life Member of Zeta Phi Beta Sorority, Incorporated.

RUN YOUR RACE AND NO ONE ELSE'S

"Education is the way to move mountains, to build bridges, and to change the world."

- Oprah Winfrey

Introduction

The question is often asked, what occurrence leads someone to earn a doctorate degree? The simple answer is, "It depends on the person!" The circumstances which dictate the precarious and arduous decision to pursue and the dedication and tenacity to complete a doctorate degree vary by an individual's experience. My personal journey to a doctorate occurred as such. I desired to be an attorney from the age of seven years old until the age of twenty-two. Toward the end of my undergraduate career, I decided not to attend law school because of an undesired headache that frustrated me and overshadowed my lifelong dream. However, what then appeared as a dream cast aside rose a new desire and plight in the area of public administration.

A trusted advisor enlightened me that many of the daily activities I engaged in as a student leader pointed in the direction of public administration and public policy. Thus, I shifted my focus and changed my goals; law school was no longer on my mind, but I would instead pursue a Master of Public Administration (M.P.A.) degree. Therefore, within a couple of years of completing my Bachelor of Arts degree from The University of Missouri (Columbia), I took the GRE and applied to the program, and here is where the course completely shifted. I was rejected. Heartbroken and feeling dejected, I accepted an invitation to a personal pity party and attended for 24 hours, after which I determined it was not the place to be and quickly sought the nearest exit.

Upon exiting the state of rejection and disparagement, my new goal was to find a comparable program at an accredited university. Program found. Mission accomplished. I went through the typical steps of filling out the forms for additional information and engaging with an admissions rep. To my dismay, the feedback received was that my undergrad GPA was too low and that I was not far enough removed from my undergraduate degree to consider my application for the program. I was advised to attend a community college in New Mexico or somewhere in the Southwest United States to elevate my GPA and then apply later. After speaking with another admissions rep who encouraged me to apply anyway, a decision was made. Accepted! What component got me in, you ask? Coincidentally enough, it was the essay. The strength of my writing carried me to the start of this new path. The path that was unbeknownst to me would end at another school two degrees later, adorned with the credentials of Dr. Khandicia Randolph.

After completing the M.P.A., it seemed natural to apply for the Ph.D. in Public Policy with a specialization in law. The rationale was an individual compromise replete with the attempt to convince me and only me that it was a sufficient substitute for the previous lifelong dream of attending law school. After a few classes, my performance declined due to my health, and this dropped my GPA below the financial aid eligibility requirement. Unable to finance the degree myself, the dream was deferred. Several years later, a yearning to complete what was started grew within. However, after careful consideration, there was zero desire to attend the previous institution. I looked into other schools and programs, including HBCUs. I was hard-pressed to find exactly what I thought I was looking for without relocating. Haphazardly, Regent University entered my sphere of influence and became an emerging target on my radar after seeing a graduation announcement from a Sorority Sister.

Researching the school and its program I found would not yield a Ph.D. in Public Policy program, but there was the opportunity to attain an M.A. in Law from their law school. I asked tentatively: Am I crazy enough to entertain the thought of a second Master's degree solely to fulfill a long-forgotten childhood dream? Nevertheless, after consulting God, myself, and one other person the answer soon proved to be, "Absolutely!" Insanity was definitely mine to have and to hold. Thus began a divinely ordained detour. During the second semester of the program, as I was fasting with my church and seeking God for what was next academically and professionally, the notion of starting a consulting firm was bequeathed to me. It was that notion that led the search for other academic programs at Regent, and I was surprised to find a Doctorate in Strategic Leadership with a concentration in global consulting from their School of Business and Leadership. The next step in my Doctoral journey was revealed to me.

Life Before My Doctorate Program

The immediate two years preceding becoming a doctoral student or becoming one again, although they were academic-ridden, were not nearly as all-consuming as life became once I was a full-time doctoral student. Yes, there were forty hours of work, reading, studying, tests, homework, and research…hmmm…perhaps those years were pretty intense; nevertheless, they pale drastically compared to what awaited me. Notwithstanding the lesser intensity of rigor, those two years did help mold the necessary thought paradigm and discipline to work full-time and simultaneously attend school full-time. Notable differences between the pre-doctorate life and being a doctoral student were my social time and free time. I would have savored more moments alone and with friends, had I known the rigor of what awaited me in my academic journey three years later.

I was immensely naive. About what? Concisely put the immense rigor, fortitude, and resilience it took to complete a doctorate degree. Put starkly, I was arrogant, or as my doctoral chair told my mother at graduation, I didn't lack confidence. I recall one incident where a fraternity brother of mine whom I had known since high school was completing his Doctorate in Ministry as I was finishing my M.A. in Law degree. One Saturday morning, he expressed with passionate discontent his utter frustration with school. This was not the first or only time. I possessed an uncanny ability to calm him, so usually I could talk him down from the proverbial ledge. Put a pin in it; we will discuss the ledge in the next section. This time, the attempt to offer comfort and empathy was an epic fail and met with hostility and an accusatory retort of "You don't understand." Being the (overly) confident person I am, his disparagement was met and raised with disdain. "How dare you sling the accusation of not understanding," was my rebuttal. After all, we were both getting our third degree. Unbeknownst to me, in that moment and period of time, he was correct. Understanding and comprehension were not my fortitudes in that situation, nor were they within my possession. It was not until later, in the thick of the struggle, that I too would go through the disparagement he was experiencing in that situation. I too would wallow in it for a period of time, and I too had to find a way to escape it. I never apologized for the way I diminished his feelings that day. It is probably time to rectify that.

A pivotal component of what life was like before beginning my doctorate degree came in determining the program. As recanted above, I was divinely led to the Doctor of Strategic Leadership program and would later come to find out during the journey I was divinely placed in the program for peculiar reasons. Nonetheless, it remained my obligation to perform due diligence and ensure that the program's composition worked for my future goals. To be clear, that future goal was not merely some narcissistic or egotistical desire to be called a "Doctor." More astutely, the goals were ensuring accreditation, that the degree was a viable terminal degree, mainly an online program, and would equip me with the educational, programmatic, and applicable knowledge required to have a consulting company and career advancement. However, these goals became secondary as I went through the program.

Upon speaking with an admission rep, it was confirmed that the degree was a terminal degree equivalent to that of a Ph.D. in that sense. Assuredly it was accredited. There were some on-campus requirements, but they were minimal. There was also an assurance that the program and subject matter taught was more applicable than theoretical and research-based. In Layman's terms, the rep said there was not as much reading, writing, and researching.

Notwithstanding having reached the finish line and completing my degree, I would like to go back and find that rep who assuredly guaranteed me there was less rigorous reading, writing, and researching involved in a doctoral pursuit. That was a lie. Should anyone try to convince you otherwise, listen not! Nonetheless, I felt assured that the degree program aligned with my goals and educational values, so I applied. The rest is, as they say, history.

Indeed, life before becoming a doctorate student was less intense. I had more time, space, and capacity for things such as going out with friends, going to movies, and sleeping. In October of 2018, there was a swift and definitive change to that cadence and lifestyle. The two years prior to the beginning of my doctoral studies found me working on my second Master's degree from law school. The practice of reading and studying was already present with a well-set stage, or so I presumed. I recall the rigor and challenges imposed upon me in that degree program, gaining a newfound respect for anyone with a J.D. (Doctorate of Juris Prudence Degree). It appeared in those moments, especially during my first semester and when contract law reared its daunting head, that the subject matter might defeat me and be the most arduous academic battle I would endure.

I recall a moment during my first semester in law school when I began to have trouble reading the texts for my first set of courses. I had to read the exact same words three times to comprehend. After performing a self-assessment which entailed questioning my intellectual ability and capacity, I sent an email to the professor asking if the mental defect occurring was normal and if I possessed the necessary abilities and competencies to meet the tasks required by this degree.

To my surprise, he answered that he had felt the same way his first semester, and his feelings of doubt and uncertainty were compounded by the fact that he uprooted his family for the pursuit. Reminiscing, the habit of emailing and heavily engaging professors was a consistent theme throughout that degree and increased exponentially over the course of my doctorate program. Despite the imputation of austerity and whatever modicum of valor it took to walk into the manifestation of a thirty-year-long forgotten dream of graduating from law school, it is still profusely dissimilar when I consider the ardent and laborious expedition that lay in wait.

Far gone were my days that were occupied with community engagement activities such as scholarship teas, volunteering at the food bank, making cards for nursing home residents, spontaneous weekend trips, and other activities. In a moment, it all changed. Freedom became a foreign word and concept.

Life as a Doctoral Student

Before beginning this section, let us consider the proper chronological context of when I finished my second Master's degree, and when the plight for the finale, as I called it, began. Graduation from Regent University was on May 12, 2018. On May 11, the Law School commissioned its graduates in a separate ceremony. Understanding the assignment, or so it was thought, the next step was to apply for the Doctor of Strategic Leadership program. June came, and the application was submitted. With ease, I was accepted. The plan was to take the remainder of the year off and begin the program in the Spring semester, which started in January. As with the themes throughout the chapter, that all changed upon receiving a call in August from the advising office after I paid the enrollment fee offering me to start in the second half of the fall semester because a few seats were left in one of my first courses. As stated, sanity is apparently not my forte; therefore, I consented and ended my brief academic hiatus sooner than anticipated.

Please understand that sooner than I anticipated was not at the start of the course; it was the moment I said "yes". Granting permission to begin two and a half months sooner meant applying for financial aid, getting registered and acclimated to the requirements, ordering books, and accepting friend requests from people on social media because they were the director of your program. It also meant attempting and, to some degree, succeeding and failing to map out my calendar to plan for assignment due dates and read in advance. Finally, what I perhaps failed at the most was the jaded attempt to wrap my mind around the varied nuances and complex amalgamation that would encapsulate my life for the next four years and, in some ways, henceforth.

Two weeks before the beginning of my first course, I reached out to my professor via email. Albeit my program was mainly via an online platform, I made it my priority to engage with the professors to get what needed from the course and the professor. This theme was consistent throughout my program, faculty engagement, and with some more than others. If space allowed, there were a myriad of anecdotes to recount about my experiences as a doctoral student, but it doesn't. Thus, my intent is to highlight the ones to be believed of more importance that would cause negligence and remiss should I not. Nevertheless, this one tidbit is too rich not to share.

In the two weeks before class started it seemed a no-brainer to start reading for class. This juncture is also the point where I reviewed the syllabus and contacted the professor. Full transparency here: I wanted to drop out the moment I read the syllabus. It was TOO much! It wasn't the professor or the course in particular but rather the demand, expectation, and vigor. My parent's enthusiasm and emotional connection to the idea of their daughter becoming a doctor kept me from quitting before I started. So, I stayed. Fortunately, it all worked out pretty well. Albeit not without tears, sleepless nights, missed meals, challenging moments, worry, doubt, a little absurdity, and a huge adjustment period.

Throughout the first semester of my program, and possibly a little longer, I basically lived at Starbucks. Life had become such that I left work and went there. I got up on the weekends and headed for coffee and a table, so often that a friend met me one day just to hang out. That was my version of quality time at the moment. The adjustment period was rough. Essentially, I put myself on lockdown for the first nine to twelve months. You wouldn't see me out in public if it weren't for school, work, the doctor, or something necessary like the pharmacy. I vividly remember my first semester and being famished but needing to continue through a book. The compromise was bacon and reading while it cooked on the stove, flipping pages while flipping bacon. The doctoral experience taught me how to say "no" and choose myself and my needs over others at the appropriate time. The pattern of being heavily involved in organizations and putting others before self was routine, but in January 2019, it came to a screeching halt. Though I had successfully completed the first course, life had already begun to pass by, yet there came a definitive moment when I resigned from everything but school, work, and family—a hard decision, yet necessary. Eventually, I learned to squeeze in the occasional dinner if there was appropriate and sufficient planning and no mitigating factors.

Here's a piece of advice, don't be arrogant. At the onset of my doctoral journey, I was academically arrogant and had to be convicted and humbled by God. Subsequently, I had to apologize to the professor I had the first semester after the conviction hit. Ultimately, she would become my doctoral chair and the single most crucial academic influence along the journey, thus making my apology extremely critical. It wasn't the presumption of "knowing-it-all" that created the fallacy but more the attitude of an academic high from the previous degree coupled with some semi-entitlement syndrome. But the behavior was fixed very quickly; nevertheless, I have gratitude that flows even from that chastisement and experience. If there are no "ouch" moments along the journey, perhaps you aren't being stretched enough.

To that end, let us focus on the idea that earning a doctorate degree is a journey, not a destination. The phrase was repeated ad nauseam during our first residency. For those unfamiliar with the idea, the residency was an immersive classroom-style learning experience for the better portion of a week. It is on campus, meals are provided, and you are forced to interact with strangers. To me, it seemed like a social experiment, and I hate social experiments. We were required to attend one at the beginning of year one and year two. Though listening to the rhetoric about the journey was not on my agenda, and emphatically I retorted it was most certainly a destination. It had a definitive beginning and end, one marked by courses, semesters, and graduation dates, all of which were mapped out. However, by the end of year one, I came to fully understand and even embrace that it was, in fact, a journey, so much so that I emailed my first professor and admitted my fault and obstinance. The journey is designed to push you, pull you, stretch you, enlarge you, at some points, shrink you, and mold you. It should be transformative in some way; arguably, it must.

There is a proverbial bridge or ledge often mentioned when discussing the day-to-day challenges of life. The phrase "don't jump" is possibly more real than ever before. Equally as real is the ledge or bridge for doctoral students. It is a physical, emotional, and mental manifestation of the frustration and challenges of the journey, and so is wanting to take that leap or metaphorically taking it. Some catalysts to such a disposition include lack of sleep leading to delirium, frustrating experiences with professors, putting your all into an assignment or paper, and receiving subpar feedback. Other scenarios include hassles with the Institutional Review Board (I.R.B.), who review your studies and ensure they comply with all regulations dealing with using human subjects in research. For some, these conflicts can lead to imposter syndrome, and for others, overconfidence. In whatever way the issues manifest, stay away from the ledge, don't jump. Should you jump, have someone who will jump in and save you. I have jumped. I took on too much as a first-year student trying to be an overachiever. It caused a severe lack of sleep, and I plummeted. When frustration with professors was at an all-time high, I had to be pulled back from the ledge. When foolishly, perfection was the goal over excellence and learning, I almost jumped. But, like me, if you jump, get up, dust yourself off, sleep, have a meal, and refocus.

Speaking of frustration, when it came to selecting a chair for my final doctoral project, which I did at the beginning of year two, God knows He frustrated me, or perhaps it was I who frustrated God with my stubbornness. The paradox of the situation was I already knew who I was supposed to ask and hoped they consented. However, in true Khandicia fashion, running seemed like a better option because I didn't want those "problems." By problems, I mean someone who would accept nothing short of exceptional, and push me to do my very best, even if I was unsure of what that was. I went so far as to attempt to get another answer from God by asking for someone else's recommendation. Looking back, all I can do is laugh. I intentionally selected a doctoral chair whom I thought would challenge and stretch me, although initially, it was the scariest thought. But I knew I wanted to be better on the other side of the journey, and I am so very grateful I did. Don't take the easy way out. Be open to being challenged by the right people for your growth and development.

Life Happens! A lot of life happens while earning a doctorate degree. You may start a job or quit a job. Sickness befalls you or your family. I've seen people lose their parents while earning the degree, and when I would have stopped, they kept going. I figured if they had the courage to proceed, then the least I could do was encourage and uphold them. There will be hellish days in your professional life. Some professors will be understanding, while others will not. Life alone is hard, compound it with the rigor and demands of a doctorate degree, and some days it is darn near impossible. Then COVID-19 hit and shut down the world. Everything we had come to know about life changed in an instant! But remember, life is going to happen. It will do what it does regardless of your status in life. Push through, even if you can't take the necessary reprieve. However, understand that pursuing academia at the highest level is not intended to be easy and requires some measure of sacrifice. That sacrifice is not limited to the student but also affects the village they comprise. So, let life happen and resolve that your determination will steady the storm. Because ultimately, you can't outlive life.

If there is one undeniable thing that occurred during life as a doctoral student, it was my transformation. I didn't only become more intelligent, integrate the perpetual use of the words posit, postulate, and proffer, or become a subject matter expert in leadership. I also found the courage to quit my job, where I had worked the majority of my adult life, to finish school as expected, choosing my needs over theirs. Although a somewhat scary decision, it was the best one I could have made. There were unexpected transformations as well. God unhardened my heart and let a few people in, both faculty and students. At the conclusion of the journey, I had some people who had become family. Most astoundingly, I learned the purpose of my being at Regent to complete that degree at the appointed time. God sent me to someone so that I could bring about their healing and restoration, a job I took with the utmost reluctance. But it was the purpose for me to be there for them as a reflection of God's love. It was simultaneously remarkable and scary to be utilized for such a purpose. During the transformative journey, I learned the importance of humility and that I wasn't "there" yet. I continued to uphold my convictions and meet the challenges head-on. It's okay to say no and prioritize your needs, whatever they may be, and choose yourself over others. I also learned to trust the process and that, indeed, it was a journey. One that climaxed at 11:32 am CDT on March 22, 2022, when I first heard, "Good afternoon, Dr. Randolph!"

Life After Becoming a Doctor

Not being extremely far removed from the days when I slept with textbooks, or old white guys as I often joked, and my laptop. Sometimes it feels like a lifetime ago, almost a sonnet-like dream. Then there are days when people and aspects of the doctoral degree pursuit of life still infiltrate actual dreams. In those moments, I want nothing more than to awaken from those dreams swiftly. But then again, the same desire existed when I was a doctoral student. Initially, as I thought about this section, it appeared that perhaps there was not a wealth of information to divulge as I am only a year removed from graduation. As I typed these words this time last year, I had yet to receive clearance on my degree. Of course, there were more superficial reliefs such as going to movies for the first time in four years, watching more television, going out with friends more, and sleeping more, all for which I am grateful, especially for the sleep. However, not all of these thoughts were just superficial, some aspects of celebration and adjustment to life after the doctoral program were superficial but necessary, prudent, and incumbent, a deeper delve into the annals of my mind revealed just how much had transpired in my life after just one short year post-graduation.

To keep things light, for now, let's discuss the pomp and circumstance of it all. Most of my immediate family traveled to Virginia Beach for the festivities during graduation week. My brother (in-law) and sister captured two photo shoots for me. My brother (in-law) being the photographer and videographer, was perfect. They both made sure I took time to capture and celebrate the moment and for that, I am perpetually grateful. Looking back on those pictures, especially the one captured as I put on full regalia for the first time, they continue to evoke every describable and indescribable emotion I felt in that moment, the moments leading up to it, and the ones to follow. Additionally, it was quite a luxury having my own photographer at both the commissioning and the graduation ceremony. Make sure you take time to celebrate the moment.

In addition to a photo shoot on campus and at the beach, I had the opportunity to have breakfast with my doctoral chair. There was immense significance in having some intimate time with her at the completion of the journey, as she had been there for the entire production. Hearing her acknowledge me as "Dr. Randolph" in person messed me up. Even hearing, her say it still sounds so strange to me when we communicate. There is a wonderment of "Who is she talking to?" Speaking of wonderment, I remain in awe every single day that God allows me to occupy this space. To be transparent, it isn't the ego trip that I am a Doctor; more conversely, it is the astounding amazement and admiration that God exceeded my expectations during and after my journey.

The ability to travel was my great fortune after hearing the coveted words "Good afternoon, Dr. Randolph." For my birthday two weeks later, Cozumel was my portion. Then about two weeks after graduation came the celebration trip to Dubai and the Maldives. In August I took another trip to Jamaica. Traveling internationally is a passion of mine. Seeing the world teaches us so much about others and ourselves. As an autonomous learner, broadening my world through travel the hunger to chase after the elusive notion of continual scholarship.

Fast forward to the holiday season, November found me in the kitchen actually helping with Thanksgiving dinner, watching part of Macy's Thanksgiving parade with my family, and enjoying other quality moments. In December, the simplicity of watching television for elongated and undetermined periods with my family even caused my mother to comment that something was different. The difference was my presence. For the previous six holiday seasons, I was a student. There was always a laptop somewhere, and in the most recent four, the laptop was joined by books, incoherent ramblings, and frustration. Being fully integrated into my family, not having to rotate between them and my computer, and being fully present is an invaluable gift. Nevertheless, as thoughts came to me about what to write for this section of the manuscript and I pondered the intimate and not-so-intimate details of my life for the past 12-14 months, it hit me like a ton of textbooks. Inarguably, there have been some wonderful times since becoming a doctor with infinite more ahead, but there have also been heartbreaking moments.

In the 12 months since completing the finale, I have suffered some tremendous losses. A cousin died in June, a very dear friend died unexpectedly at the end of August, one of my sister-friend's mother passed in November, whom I had known since my freshman year of college, and on June 22 of that same year, my grandma left. It had been three months to the date that I received the call that the title of doctor was mine when she went from labor to reward. She had, however, kept her portion of our agreement. I agreed to complete the degree and become the family's first doctor, and in turn, she agreed to hang around until it was complete.

The pain of loss is necessary to acknowledge because, since their departures, in the infancy of my being a doctor, there are milestones I wish I could share with them, like being a published author, which is a direct product of my doctorate degree. Gratitude is still my portion, as they all did see me complete my journey, and my solace remains resolute in that alone.

Turning the attention from the personal anecdotes of my post-doctoral journey, let us briefly examine a more generalized theme, the adjustment period. Every person I have conversed with regarding life after becoming a doctor resonates with a similar or identical theme of adjusting to life without the demand and rigor of the degree. Personally, it was akin to being under a rock for four years and, without notice, emerging into the brave new world. You begin to understand just how all-consuming being a doctoral student was in every finite aspect of your life. Even in writing this manuscript, the challenges of using a first-person tone and conjunctions cause me uneasiness. Intentionally there is a concerted deliberateness to veer away because, for four years, A.P.A. was King/Queen. For some, there is even social awkwardness after the impacting self-isolation that occurred, exacerbated by COVID-19. Fortunately, the time exists that recreational reading has become part of my cadence as well as cooking more.

From a professional viewpoint, earning a doctorate degree did not guarantee immediate career elevation or change. As someone who chose to leave my former employer to focus solely on school and my final project in my last year to ensure timely graduation, navigating the job market has been daunting. Though many employers consented not to bet on me, I bet on myself. The results of that bet are not only my inclusion in this manuscript as a contributing author but also the release of my first published book this year entitled *The Black American Church: Leadership Dispensation and Challenges* and co-authored a textbook chapter entitled *The Implications of Race and Culture on Followership* with my brother and fellow Doctor of Strategic Leadership. The book is my final doctoral project in complete manuscript form and has broken into the top hundred of its category on Amazon. I committed to textbook authorship while on my graduation trip halfway around the world. Apparently, the adjustment period had yet to be ignited. I have also appeared on the podcast, *Well Written* which targets graduate students, *The Doc Chat, Horizons Author Lounge,* and *The Leadership Toolkit.* Other projects on the list will be birthed at the appropriate time. Where they fall on the horizon is yet to be determined. One certainty is that even after being a doctoral student, the impact and influence of scholastic achievement remain paramount in my daily walk.

DR. SAMARIA R. ROBERTS-WASHINGTON

Dr. Samaria R. Washington is a Licensed Nursing Home Administrator. She specializes in Skilled Nursing and Rehabilitation, Assisted Living, policy analysis, staff education, governmental regulations, with over 25 years of experience. Her current role involves multi-facility operations management. She has developed growth and expansion projects to include ventilator units, dialysis service, and person-centered care facility improvements. She has a proven record of cultivating positive community relations internally and externally with private and government agencies. She is actively involved with healthcare providers in all settings and referral sources. She is the current chair of the DC Health Care Association.

Dr. Washington earned her Doctor of Healthcare Administration from Virginia University of Lynchburg.

I AM MY SISTER AND BROTHER'S KEEPER

"You have to stay in school. You have to. You have to go to college. You have to get your degree. Because that's the one thing people can't take away from you is your education. And it is worth the investment."

- Michelle Obama

Introduction

I had my last child and only daughter four days before I turned forty years old. I quickly realized that I would not be able to retire for a very long time. I started my career as a Respiratory Therapist. I eventually transitioned into marketing and ultimately became a Licensed Nursing Home Administrator. Being a licensed nursing home administrator is a rewarding but extremely stressful job. I absolutely love what I do, though I am concerned with the state of the industry. That's why I decided that I needed to become more active and intentional in ensuring that the next generation of long-term care leaders are properly prepared to advance our industry.

Retirement will look unconventional for me. I fancy myself doing interim administrator roles a few months out of the year and spending the remainder of the year doing speaking engagements, legal case consulting, and teaching aspiring healthcare leaders. My preference would be to do some of that teaching from a beautiful beach on a tropical island via my laptop.

I am a first-generation college graduate and the only member of my immediate family to become a doctor. My great Aunt Emma used to encourage me to go to school to be a teacher or a nurse back in the seventies. Back then, they were among the few professions at which African Americans women could make a good living. She was so proud when I told her that I didn't become a nurse, but I did become a respiratory therapist. She looked confused at first, so I described it as a nurse that helps people with breathing problems. Though she was suffering with an advanced stage of dementia at the time, when I told her about my profession, she lit up like a Christmas tree!

My mom (Cora Lee) lived long enough to see me earn my bachelor's and master's degrees. She knew that I was pursuing my doctorate. She was so proud and would tell anyone who would listen about my accomplishments. I wanted to be a source of pride for my family, but more importantly an inspiration to my younger relatives, especially my children. I think it's working. So far, my first-born Raymond, is all but dissertation away from attaining his PhD in Mathematics and Informatics. My second son Arrington is a rising sophomore majoring in Business Administration and Marketing. My youngest and only daughter Morgan is a rising 7th grader, but apparently wants to be a boss like her mom. I have a host of younger cousins that are killing the higher education game!

My mother was born on the Livingston Plantation in Monticello, Florida. I was fortunate enough to be able to visit her childhood home before it was demolished. Seeing where my mother was born left a lasting impression on me. I was able to share the experience with my youngest son. I have always worked hard to provide for my family and shield them from some of the unpleasant experiences I had. Seeing the humble beginnings of my mother reignited my desire to leave a legacy and a blueprint of success for my family.

Life before Doctorate Program

I got married to my high school sweetheart the same week I graduated from high school. He was in the army and stationed in Missouri. Within the week I was relocating to St. Louis, Missouri. My oldest child was born in Missouri a few months before we were transferred to Frankfurt, Germany. While we were in Germany, I met a neighbor who was a respiratory therapist. I would see her at the hospital where we worked together and one day, she explained what she exactly she did for her job. When my first marriage began to unravel, I started looking for my own pathway to success. I left Germany and went back home to Miami. At first, I wanted to become a nurse. Trying to get into nursing school was a challenge. There were long wait lists and a list of pre-requisites before you would even be considered for admission to a nursing program. I was about to become a single parent and needed to figure out how I was going to take care of myself and my son. I didn't have time for waiting lists and prerequisites. I eventually enrolled in a technical school where I completed training to become a Respiratory Therapist. This was one of the best decisions of my life. I met one of my dearest friends while in the respiratory therapy program. Her name was Cynthia, and we are friends to this day.

After completing the program and passing my boards, I began working as a respiratory therapist immediately. I started to feel anxious about the end of my marriage and my separation from the military community. So, I decided to join the Army myself. Because I was already a respiratory therapist, I was given a sign on bonus, allowed to choose my first duty station, and was only required to complete basic training before transitioning to my first duty station. I chose Walter Reed in Washington, DC because my estranged husband was stationed in Virginia. I thought it would allow us to be able to co-parent our son better. I fell in love with the DC metropolitan area otherwise known as the DMV. While working at Walter Reed, I moonlighted at several area hospitals to supplement my income. I made significantly more money working with the agencies than I did in the army. I met some amazing people there who encouraged me to go back to school and pursue my dreams. After I was honorably discharged from the army, I decided to stay in the DMV. I found my passion while working in nursing homes in the suburbs of Maryland, just outside of Washington, DC, and decided to become a Nursing Home Administrator.

While married to my second husband, I went back to school to obtain a bachelor's in science with a Healthcare specialization. It was one of the busiest times of my life. I was working full-time as an Admissions Director in a nursing home and raising my son and stepdaughter. My husband worked for the federal government and traveled a lot. Since he was gone roughly two weeks a month, I was the primary caregiver for the children. Through it all, I managed to complete my bachelor's in science to become a first-generation college graduate. I thought that a new degree would come with a raise and promotion. That was not the case. When I asked my Regional Director of Operations about getting into the Administrator in Training (AIT) program to become a Nursing Home Administrator, he recommended that I get a master's degree. That's when I enrolled in an accelerated MBA program at Columbia Union College (now Washington Adventist University). I recalled the words from Isaiah, "No weapon formed against me shall prosper". In fact, I was in the first graduating class of the accelerated program. The first week of class I found out that I was expecting my second child. My husband tried to discourage me from pursuing my MBA at the time. Initially, I thought he was concerned about my wellbeing due to the pregnancy. I quickly realized that he was more concerned about me surpassing his education level.

I've never been one to allow others to deter me from my goals. By my calculations, I would deliver my precious baby about three months before completing the program. I decided to take the full 12 weeks maternity leave so I could complete the program prior to returning to work. I moved my mother to Maryland from Miami to help me with the children so I could finish school. I figured that once I had the baby it would be harder to go back to school. My boss at the time terminated my assistant while I was out on maternity leave and subsequently asked me to return to work prior to the end of my twelve weeks leave. It was hard working full time, caring for a newborn, and being enrolled in an accelerated graduate program. Charlene, one of my best friends, was the Director of Social Services at my facility. She was unbelievably supportive during my pregnancy and my master's program. I think I cried in her office almost daily throughout the program. She would always offer words of encouragement and most importantly snacks! She kept all kinds of snacks in her office. Until this very day, she tells me how proud she is of my accomplishments. My mother cared for my son while I went back to work and finished my degree. I still did not get into the Administrator in Training program at that time. I decided to move on to another organization. After a year at my new organization, I tried to get into their AIT program. I didn't make it into their program either. The AIT program has been a coveted and elusive program for many years. The lack of availability and reasonable compensation makes becoming a Nursing Home Administrator unobtainable for many. After about two years, I started looking for other AIT opportunities.

We decided to build our dream home to accommodate our growing family and careers. Having my mom nearby was a blessing. This also meant that I had one more person to take care of. As luck would have it, my second marriage was unraveling. It wasn't all because of my educational or career endeavors, but that was a big part of it. As I continued to aspire to further my education and career, my spouse became more and more distant. I found out about an undeniable indiscretion that would ultimately lead to the dissolution of our marriage. I couldn't just leave. I had to devise a plan that would allow me the ability to be able to care for me and my children. That would require professional and personal growth. I began to get serious about my search for an AIT program. I became more determined than ever to become an Administrator and live my life on my own terms.

I learned a lot about myself during this time. I realized that I did not have the time or desire to be with a man that was insecure. I didn't have time to tell someone constantly how handsome they were, how smart they were, or any other number of compliments. I was sick of hearing about what a catch my husband was because of his salary, education, and appearance. He lacked other qualities that were more important like loyalty, patience, selflessness, and just being a supportive spouse. I was tired of playing amateur detective. I was tired of waiting for things to get better. From that time on, I decided that I had to be the source of my own happiness.

Life during Doctorate Program

I was selected as an Administrator in Training program through a nationwide search with Medical Facilities of America (MFA) in Roanoke, Virginia. The AIT program required that I relocate to Roanoke, Virginia for a month for intensive training by the leaders of MFA. We were able to go home on the weekends. After the initial 30 days in Roanoke, I was assigned to a facility in Chesapeake, Virginia. The program would be the beginning of my nursing home administrator career. It would also help me prepare to walk away from a marriage that was stifling my growth. This is where my doctoral journey began. I met Lakesha while in the AIT program, who would become another close friend and also introduce me to a doctoral program.

I originally started out as a PH.D. student. The program was based upon the concept of Knowledge Ara Modules (KAM) which is a model where the courses are self-studied and self-paced. . The first step in the program was to complete a Professional Development Plan that would be reviewed and approved by university faculty. The plan would be my guide for my program completion. The program required continuous enrollment while you completed a KAM on a particular topic. Each KAM would take approximately 6 months to a year to complete. Each semester also required me to complete a short report on my activities during the semester. The program included several residency courses that were four or five days long. The residencies were held in different locations around the country and abroad. I came to find that this was not the right format for me. Unfortunately, I had already spent years of my life and tens of thousands of dollars chasing my dream of becoming a doctor. I went from semester to semester with little progress. I eventually stopped attending and had all but given up on pursuing my doctorate.

A couple of years after I stopped my Ph. D. program, I was contacted about a new program with my old university. The new program was a Doctor of Business Administration with a Healthcare Administration specialization which seemed perfect for me now that I was a practicing Nursing Home Administrator. This program included nine courses, several residencies, and the doctoral study process. I completed the coursework with no problems. The doctoral study was a different story. No one on my committee had the experience required to understand the topic of my doctoral study. I was studying the correlation between nursing home administrator turnover and the correlation to quality of care in nursing homes. Semester after semester, I would go back and forth with my committee. It was a classic example of two steps forward and one step back. Amid this back and forth, I got divorced, cared for my dying mother, got remarried, had a child, and buried my mother. I was exhausted and defeated. The program may have been perfect for me, but the school was not. After losing my mom and primary support system, I was discouraged and gave up. I took another break from my doctoral journey.

One day while scrolling on Facebook, I saw an ad for a new Doctor of Healthcare Administration program starting at

Virginia University of Lynchburg in Lynchburg, Virginia. I scrolled past it a few times before I decided to investigate it. It sounded too good to be true. I called the university and ended up speaking with Dr. Gupta. He seemed very knowledgeable and invested in my situation. He convinced me to enroll in the program. I had a very tight timeline to complete the application process because the inaugural DHA program was going to start in a matter of a couple of weeks or so. Somehow, I managed to get everything together and started the final leg in my journey to become a doctor. It was not easy.

The COVID-19 pandemic had moved class environments from in-person to online when I was enrolled in the program. It consisted of online course work and Saturday zoom sessions with our professors and classmates. The courses followed the typical model of online courses. We had weekly assignments that included several weekly postings that included a reading assignment, answering questions, and responding to our professors and peers. I really enjoyed the weekend zoom sessions. The professors gave lectures where we had the opportunity to interact with the professor and each other. There were also weekly assignments and projects.

As if being in a doctoral program was not enough, I had a fall at work that fractured and dislocated my shoulder. It was my dominant shoulder and this made completing my assignments quite challenging. I used a speech recognition program called Dragon to transcribe my assignments. I managed to keep up and do very well. I continued to work and care for my family as I recovered from my injuries. I endured a series of therapy sessions before my physician determined that I was ready to have surgery to repair the multiple injuries to my shoulder. I had surgery during my final semester in the program. The final semester of the program was based on group assignments where everyone was randomly placed in a group of four or five students based on our last names.

My team consisted of a total of four students because we were the last four students in our cohort. Together, we completed a teaching, leadership, and research practicum. We also did a short internship at local organizations. My favorite part of the program was our teaching practicum which was to create an online course. Being the overachievers that we were, we created an entire school! Complete with a mascot. I was surprised at how well the project turned out. Though it was a stressful amount of work, the process was equally as fun. My team supported me through my surgery and recovery. I was only down for about a week before I was back at it. We were so proud of our finished product. Even though we generally worked well together, there is always at least one person that does not pull their weight. Our team was no different. We were determined not to allow one person to bring down the entire team. We worked a little harder to help our teammate and subsequently helped ourselves. My professors were also very supportive and allowed me extra time to complete my individual assignments that were due the week I had surgery. I would not have been able to finish on time without the support of my professors and classmates.

Life of Completing the Doctorate Degree & Life now as a Doctor

The ink was probably still wet on my new degree when I started my new job as the Regional Director of Operations for Bridge Point Healthcare. While my position does not require a doctoral degree, it puts me in circles with many other individuals who have terminal degrees. The skilled nursing facilities I support are in Washington, DC. The leaders in the district are very respectful of credentials and recognize educational accomplishments. I don't demand or beg to be recognized as Dr. Washington, it's given freely. I am proud to work in an environment that is filled with professional and highly educated people of color. There is no lack of role models in Washington, DC.

Finishing my doctorate was the highlight of my educational career. It coincided with a major change in my professional career. My new role involves multifacility management. I love working in the facility and being close to the residents and their families. One of the things that drew me to the profession was the ability to affect change and help people. I am now able to help more people than ever. I am the chair of the District of Columbia Healthcare Association (DCHCA), which is a trade association that represents nursing homes and assisted living facilities in Washington, DC. I try to assist our industry leaders any way I can. My goal is to reach across agencies and organizations to bring about positive change to our industry. It requires a lot of time, effort, and meetings. We are experiencing unprecedented changes in the long-term care industry. We must adapt to survive and thrive so that we can continue to care for one of the most vulnerable populations. I have always felt a sense of responsibility to leave my industry better than I found it. That includes educating and mentoring the next generation of healthcare leaders.

I am also an approved vendor for Maryland's 80 hour Assisted Living Manager (ALM) course. This is the entry level course to prepare individuals to become assisted living managers in an assisted living facility. I am passionate about this program because it is an opportunity for people to move into leadership roles and open their own assisted living facilities. It fills my heart to help someone break generational curses and become a successful entrepreneur. I personally hand pick my students to ensure that they are not in this business just for the money. Training new ALMs is a labor of love. It requires a great deal of time and effort throughout the entirety of their training. Caring for those that cannot care for themselves is similar to ministry in ways. You must have your clients' best interests at heart. That means that your profit margin may not be as high as some of your competitors. My goal is to teach my students how to take good care of their residents and still make a reasonable profit that will allow them to reinvest into their businesses.

What should be one of the happiest and most fulfilling times in my life, has been one of the most challenging. As I mentioned earlier in the chapter, not everyone that starts or joins you on your doctoral journey will make it till the end. If they make it to the end of the journey, they still might not remain in your life after the journey is completed. Some people may view the personal pursuit of your doctorate degree as a slight against them and their lack of the same credentials. I do not wield my accomplishments as a weapon against anyone nor do I use them to make anyone feel lesser. One of the people closest to me made it very clear through a series of actions that my hard work was not important and didn't mean much to them. It was bad enough that there was little to no support from them during my doctoral journey. Comments they made during my graduation weekend were insensitive and hurtful. I did what I had been doing for years, I ignored the comments and kept moving. It was the only way to deal with the years of emotional abuse. I only have one relative in the immediate area aside from my children. My girlfriends have truly become family and they love and support me unconditionally.

I packed my bags and went to attend the pre-graduation festivities with my classmates. I gifted myself a pair of red bottoms for my hard work and sacrifice. I put on my new dress and new shoes and had a ball celebrating with my classmates. Our graduation festivities included pre-graduation events and an opportunity to meet with our classmates and professors for the first time in-person before our graduation. We made it an entire weekend of fun and fellowship. We had spent countless hours on the phone and on zoom meetings. Nothing could compare to our in-person time together. We were brought together by a life-changing experience. Together, we became doctors.

After many years of chasing my dream, on August 24, 2021, I finally became Dr. Samaria R. Roberts-Washington. Since we were the inaugural class of the program, we received custom graduation regalia and the great fortune to attend an in-person graduation. The school even gave us custom graduation themed masks. It was amazing to see all my classmates with their families and friends. I was elated to have my children and family present to witness the monumental occasion. So, if you find yourself in a situation where you are not being celebrated by someone closest to you, celebrate yourself. When you're done basking in the wonder of you, then you will be able to deal with any broken situations.

DR. TRENTON WATSON

Dr. Trenton Watson obtained his Bachelor of Science degree in Communications from Tennessee State University and holds a Master's degree in Educational Leadership and Administration from Cumberland University. Dr. Watson obtained his Ph.D. in Organizational Leadership from The University of Arizona Global Campus. Dr. Watson has been an Educator in the Memphis-Shelby County Schools in Memphis, Tennessee for over 10 years and has held many roles including Vice Principal and Principal roles in the school district. Dr. Watson during his spare time enjoys traveling, public speaking, learning, and spending time with his wife and children. Dr. Watson is a Member of Kappa Alpha Psi, Fraternity Incorporated.

SHAKEN, BUT NOT DETERRED

"Don't just aspire to make a living but inspire to make a difference."
- Denzel Washington

Introduction

My grandmother was the type of person who would command attention from her kids and grandkids. It was my graduation day, and I was excited about the possibilities of the parties that night, but she was focused on my future. She sat me down on her couch and looked me in the eye and said, "Baby, take education as far as you can take it." I will never forget those words because it showed me that my future wasn't going to be trapped in a box or dictated by someone else. Moments like this shaped me to believe that I had to choose to be the best I could be so I could make my mother and grandmother proud.

The idea that a young African-American male from the north side of Memphis could be anything more than what I saw directly in front of me was challenging. Many people thought that I would end up stuck in that box that society had created for us as black males. I had to prove to myself that I could be more than a statistic. I wanted to make my family and myself proud. I was going to set the standard for others coming behind me. That's why going to college was only the beginning. I was going to be a beacon of light for others to follow.

Life before Doctorate Program

From the first day of college, I made it a point that I was going to graduate and do so on time. In the beginning, it was a struggle because I had to adjust to the fact of being on my own. After the first semester, my GPA was at 1.75. My mother was such an amazing source of motivation for me, she said "Honey, your grandmother would not approve of you losing out on your opportunity." I determined I had to refocus. I was sitting in the library that next semester when it hit me, I had to find a tutor and I had to keep myself out of the club. It was important to set some realistic goal-centered priorities for myself and physically post them where I could look at them every day. Each morning when I got out of bed, I made sure to get on my knees and look up. Each night when I went to bed, I made sure to get on my knees and look up. I posted my goals on the ceiling as I felt like my goals would be closer to God and while I was on my knees praying to Him, I wouldn't forget the people who prayed for me to be in the position I was in. Being able to dig in, I was able to see that I had to minimize my ego and turn up my expectations. Failing was not the end, but it was a call for a reset. When I understood that I needed to reset, that's when I made the Dean's List for the remaining 7 semesters of my undergraduate career. I knew from this moment going forward that I could not allow myself to be drawn into anything that was going to distract me from reaching my goal. It also taught me that true intelligence is not about having all the right answers, it's about asking the right questions and seeking the correct information.

I chose to stand firmly on what I was taught by my mother and grandmother. I felt that I owed them this much. The desire to learn had to start with me. I couldn't sit back and wait for it to fall into my lap. I had to be assertive and pursue the available opportunities. Education has so much value and is always in high demand. I wasn't going to miss out on the chance to set the standard.

From the land of Golden Sunshine stands a school on Cumberland's shore. There is a school of greater service, one that we adore. Tennessee State University gave me an opportunity to be more than I thought I could be. I learned the value of perseverance and friendship; I also re-ignited my love of life and education. From there, I began my adult journey trying to figure out my place in the world. I started out working in the business sector and thought it was where I was destined to be, but very soon I felt there was something missing. Like I had left something unfinished. I knew it was as my mother had predicted when she said that there was a calling for me in education.

I stepped into the educational realm in an unconventional way. Since I did not major in education in college, I was hired on a permit which only lasted three years. I had some expertise in English because I had taken enough classes to qualify for a minor, but I never submitted the paperwork because I was adamant that I was never going into education. I taught English 9 and 10 and I was very passionate about learning, though I started to notice that most teachers in my field had advanced degrees. So, I began to ask around about programs that would fit my schedule and would help me reach my new goals for education. Once I found the program, I was blessed to be in school with other individuals who shared similar goals and interests. This was my first introduction to a cohort. I was blown away by the different perspectives and experiences these individuals had. It helped me not only professionally but spiritually, emotionally, and even physically, as one of my cohort members was a personal trainer. I shifted my thinking again because this was not only challenging work, but it was relevant to what I was doing in the classroom. I could not wait to finish this program and use the principles and tools I learned.

When graduation arrived, I was thinking about my next steps in the academic process. I decided that I was going to get a second master's degree so that I could be an administrator. I was not going to stop the work because my mind was still in learning mode. So, I continued toward that second master's degree. The one thing I didn't consider was the toll it was taking on me and my family. After all, I was a husband and a father. I wish I had considered that more prior to committing myself to the program. Although my family was very supportive, there were several things I missed by not prioritizing them first. Since receiving the second master's degree, it has afforded me some opportunities that I couldn't see before. I am thankful that my family has extended much grace in the process of moving forward in education.

Being in the classroom was an adventure that taught me a great deal on how to appropriately inspire scholars. I say that because they inspired me as well. Each year in the classroom, I learned more and more about the learning process. It is what drives me to do the work I do. I wanted to learn continuously and never stop. I went to every conference or event I could to help improve my learning prowess. It was at a conference that I ran into a person who changed my life. Now let's get it straight, I promised my grandmother and mother that I would take education as far as I could, but at the time I was a little burned out because I had just completed two master's degrees back-to-back. As much as I was eager to learn, I wasn't so eager to jump back into that lifestyle of constant study and assignments again.

Now sitting at this conference in St. Louis, I was so intent on learning the concepts, I didn't notice the person sitting next to me. I never even took the time to look over. I took notes like a person possessed and I couldn't wait to go back and share what I had learned. On the second day of the conference, the person next to me tapped me on the shoulder and said, "Wow, you are really taking down a great deal of information." I was like "Thanks." This young lady just kept talking to me and I wasn't really interested in the conversation until finally I just stopped what I was doing and gave her the opportunity to finish her words. While she was talking to me, she dropped a message in my spirit that I won't soon forget. She stated that the education I had already received had laid the foundation for the education I was about to achieve. I was blown away because this lady didn't know me at all. But I became so intrigued by her that I made sure to sit next to her for the rest of the week. Each day she would give me more information on how I could achieve a higher level of success on my educational journey. A part of that was making sure that I started and completed the terminal level of Ph.D. The irony of that conversation is that I was already thinking about it but I had no idea how to start or what program to get into. As she was now another person who had poured into my life, I promised her that I would make sure to not only start the process but complete the terminal degree journey. After that conversation, I wasted no time in my search for the right program. I got online as soon as I got to my hotel room and began to research programs that would fit my schedule and lifestyle. I stumbled upon a University that seemed based on the advertisement to fit my schedule. They even had a representative that would be in the Memphis area to explain the program to me in person. I was so excited that I couldn't contain myself. I was looking forward to meeting the recruiter and starting the application process. At the time, I was thinking this process would be just like the master's degree process. I was so confident that this was going to be a breeze that I told my friends that if I wasn't finished in a year then I would buy them all a plane ticket to anywhere. To this day, I am still paying on that wager.

Life during Doctorate Program

When I started the doctoral journey, I was full of expectations. I felt as though this was going to be my crowning moment. I had worked all these years and reaching this terminal level of education was going to take me places professionally that I could only dream of. Even from meeting the recruiter, I was like this was going to be the best journey ever. I was in for a rude awakening. The first class was so intense that I was worried about if I was truly ready to start this journey. I was lost on a couple of assignments, and it shook me, but I said that I was not going to allow something as trivial as this to stop me from reaching my goal. I had to learn to form some good study habits all over again. I will admit that I had the advantage of keeping my focus on the educational leadership track. I thought that the focus of my master's degree study could be a great baseline for the doctoral program. Many of the classes were simply a review of things that I had studied during not only my master's degree process but also the on-the-job training I received while working in the school district. So how did this impact me? It meant that I could keep up with the lifestyle that I so loved. I was able to maintain a personal life without missing a beat, but what I didn't know was that the pre-dissertation classes were designed that way for a reason.

I wasn't prepared for what lay before me. I didn't know that this was just the calm before the storm.

The next thing I knew, the easy work I thought was not much to deal with became more and more challenging. My social calendar started to dry up. I began to miss more and more events. I found that being tired was an understatement when it came to getting work completed. I had a routine that I began to use every day once I discovered the truth. I would tell myself, "Stop being closed to the learning process. You were not placed in this position because you already know everything. You were placed in this position because you have so much more to learn." I learned through this affirmation the power of saying no to people. I had to refocus on the correct path in order to reach this milestone. Goals and milestones themselves are vital on the way to prosperity in the doctoral process. Deciding on milestones helped me process the journey better and allowed me to understand that I couldn't eat the whole elephant in just one bite.

It is critical to remember that life doesn't stop just because you are in a terminal degree program. I don't know why I felt like life was going to give me a break and slow down when I began working on this degree. I assumed that the world would suddenly stop spinning and I would be at the center of it all working on my dissertation. There was so much I still had to take care of, such as starting a new job in an upper-level administrative position at an alternative school. If that wasn't enough, I had to take care of my family, which was my number one priority. Life will continue and you must roll with the punches. If you are going to win at this level, you must be prepared to push back hard. It is an adjustment that many who step into this realm don't fully consider. It was not that I had anxiety about missing out on things, but that I feared not being at my highest level when it came to my family, friends, and job. I had to prioritize and make sure that all of my responsibilities were accounted for. The only thing about all of this is that I began to put too many irons in the fire. I took on so much that I truly started to wear myself down to submission. This did not service me well because now I had no energy left to do anything. Self-care is important and you must realize that this is a marathon of a program, not a sprint. In the marathon, you train differently. The long haul becomes the minimal goal. If you are truly in alignment with what you need, your family and friends will understand what you are doing and give you the space to accomplish the goal. Not only will they give you space, but your family and friends will offer you support when the time comes.

The value of a village goes without saying. I was blessed to be able to move through my undergraduate years without much difficulty. It laid the foundation for high-level learning. I lived to do my best so that I could make my family proud. Graduate school was a little more challenging, but I will share with you a secret, my master's level classes themselves were a breeze. It was the thesis that kicked my butt, (but don't tell my grad school professors). Back to the main point, the most important thing you can do is to remain humble and heed wise counsel. You can't do this alone. It takes having people in your corner who believe in what you are doing. It doesn't always have to be family, but it helps that the people closest to you understand the struggle. From my background growing up around educators and having an educated spouse, the process of getting support was a lot easier than it can be. Even my in-laws were all educators. What they all communicated was education is a journey to some and a destination to others. Those who choose the destination will never get frustrated with the journey. The value of that village will remind you of the power that lies within you. They will encourage you even when you are discouraging yourself. This also lends itself to the cohort you are part of while on your doctoral journey. I absolutely adored the fact that when I first entered the school, they paired me with a group of individuals who had similar interests and backgrounds. This was great because these were individuals who could understand the struggle and we could lift one another up when we moved through the learning process. Of course, there were challenges being that we were all in different parts of the country, but the comradery was established from the very beginning.

In moving through the learning process, eventually I found my groove. I was able to finish the prerequisite courses without so much as a pause. After a year and a half, it was time to transition to the dissertation process. The blessing was that our writing for each chapter had begun while we were in the prerequisite courses so that made the writing ongoing and less stressful. Each chapter that I completed was bringing me closer to my dream of being Dr. Trenton M.

Watson. I went and hired an editor to briefly look over my writing so I could make sure to polish all the details prior to turning it all in. Once I finished that proposal, I was on top of the world. The grind was well worth it. I scheduled my defense with the dissertation chair and my committee and was ready to conquer the world. I defended that proposal and got it approved. I was feeling great about this milestone. When suddenly, the bottom started to fall out. A couple of days after the defense, my dissertation chair quit the program and subsequently quit on me. I was blown away. So the university assigned another chair to me and this person immediately suggested I do my defense after they went through my proposal. I was furious and frustrated beyond measure. The new chair ripped my proposal to shreds and told me that it was not ready for anyone to listen to. So, I humbled myself and began to work on it again. Once it was up to the satisfaction of my new chair, I scheduled a defense again with the new committee.

The Saturday prior to the second defense, I got an email stating that my new chair was no longer with the university, and I would be assigned a different chair and committee. I just started laughing because I thought I was in the twilight zone. That following Monday, the new chair emailed me and asked me to send my original proposal to her. I reluctantly adhered to the request. Two days later, my newest chair said she loved the work, and I was ready to move forward. Eventually, I got an opportunity to discuss my next steps on the phone with my new chair, but wouldn't you know it, she expressed to me that she was about to leave and go to another university. I will be perfectly honest, I hung up the phone. I went through 5 dissertation chairs in a 3-month period. When I got to the last one and he asked me to basically start over, I said "I Quit!" I walked away from the program with no intention of ever going back as I felt I was robbed. I subsequently looked to file a lawsuit against the university and all those involved in the process. It was my mother who talked me out of following through because she said the stress of it all was going to be too much for me and I had other things to focus on. But she made sure to let me know that she expected me at some point to finish the job.

Life of completing the Doctorate Degree and Life as a Doctor

For a couple of years after the fallout, I went without thinking about finishing the process. I was so detached from it that I didn't care about how many times the university called me or if they were going to pay for me to return. I was so distraught, and meanwhile my career was on the rise, so I felt as though I didn't need it anyway, but it was the promise I made to my mother and grandmother that kept drawing me back. I couldn't let it go and I had to find a way to get this done. One of the things I knew for a fact is that I couldn't go back to the same program I was in before, but I was not patient enough to possibly start over. Luckily, there were talks about a dissertation completion program at a leadership conference I was attending. I spoke to this representative and he gave me an overview of how his university could help me. I admit I was hesitant, but I took the information, and I went home to ponder my next move. After consulting with my wife and kids, I decided to move forward with the process.

I was under the impression that I was just going to pick up where I left off. But the university informed me that I had to take some preliminary classes before I could get to the completion portion. I didn't want to at first but when I met the lady who would eventually become my dissertation chair, I was overly convinced. She told me that those few hours would be strictly for refreshing my mind on how to write and process. I trusted her words and worked through the classes. Once I completed those classes, I began the process to defend the proposal. I again got excited and pushed through completing the necessary chapters. I went to the residency and had an amazing time getting motivated by the department heads and other former students who had completed the program. I pushed hard and I worked tirelessly with my dissertation chair. So much so that when it was time to defend my proposal, I didn't know what to do. I didn't know what to expect, but my chair was very encouraging and helped me walk through that defense with confidence. Once it was over, the entire committee celebrated and extended their commitment to helping me drive home the research regarding the influence of school leaders on the morale and motivation of teachers. They were so impressed with my journey that they nominated me to be the first graduate of the university to deliver the commencement address during the hooding ceremony. This was the first time in the school's history that something like this had been done, and they wanted it to be me. As I was standing there giving that speech, I thought about my family, specifically my grandmother who had limited education. She believed that I would be in this position long before I was able to stand and deliver a message to the graduating class.

Today, I stand as Principal of a High School because I was able to stand on my word of not giving up on the process. The push toward finishing what I started was more than just myself but those around me. I needed my amazing wife and family to know how much I appreciated them for their support. I needed my mother to know that I never forgot the promise I made. I needed my grandmother to know that I felt her heavenly hand on my shoulder every step of the way. This process is not an easy one, but I promise you it's worth it. When you look back and reflect on the journey, if you do it with compassion and perseverance, you will appreciate it even more. God knew what I needed and how I would get there. He gave me the strength to get out of my own way and allow Him to truly guide my path. I don't know about others but as for me, if it wasn't for the Lord on my side, I don't know where I would be.

DR. ZAKIA GATES

Dr. Zakia Y. Gates is an Assistant Professor of Education at Eastern University, teaching both the undergraduate and graduate levels. Dr. Gates earned a PhD in Professional Studies in K-12 Education from Capella University in 2016. Dr. Gates has two decades of experience across various educational institutions – charter schools and higher education - including serving as Director of Education at a juvenile facility from 2007 to 2014. Dr. Gates philosophy of advancing the mission is through social responsibility, transformative pedagogy, and cultural responsiveness for all humanity. Dr. Gates footprint of this philosophy, turned research interest in critical race theory, social justice, DEIB, culturally relevant and sustaining pedagogies, and exploring the experiences of Black women in societal and educational contexts, informs her teaching practices in both undergraduate and graduate levels. Dr. Gates believes that educational spaces are movements of protests where the sole purpose of teaching is to lead future generations out of ignorance. Dr. Gates enjoys spending time with her daughter, reading, meditating, writing for personal and professional obligations, learning new languages - Japanese is her favorite, knitting, and listening to music.

PURSUE THE PATH TO INVITE COMMUNITY

"Educational progress is a national concern; education is a private one."

- Nikki Giovanni

Introduction

As I write this chapter, I am reminded of the people who came before me and paved the way for my life from before my doctorate degree to my completion. People such as my grandparents were born during a time when African Americans "had no power" and privileged groups ``had no hearts" - as actress Lynn Whitfield said in her portrayal of Josephine Baker. My parents come to mind, who still managed to find strength in the oppression to overcome the historical atrocities that were designed for them to fail. I've held on to the mantra Dr. Maya Angelou immortalized as a poem, "And still I rise". It has been a narrative I repeat to myself to fuel my determination to journey forward in my life and honor those who came before. I stand on the shoulders of my ancestors, from the cotton fields to the reconstruction, who provided a roadmap to change while enduring the systemic forms of all isms and phobias that we have today. People such as Dr. Edward Bouchet, the first African American to earn a doctorate in physics from Yale in 1876 to Dr. W.E.B. Dubois, the first African American to earn a doctorate from Harvard University in 1895. This is where the verse "the hope and dream of the slave" still rings loud and clear (Maya Angelou's poem, "And Still I Rise"). Yet, there is one person whose name does not surface when hearing stories of African American experiences of breaking through barriers in societal and academic contexts of advanced degrees. We often hear about the great men who have earned doctorates in the sciences, mathematics, and history, but where are the stories about Black women scholars and the PhD?

As I present this first part of my life before the doctorate, I would like to acknowledge the life and work of Dr. Georgiana Simpson. She was the first Black woman to earn a doctorate degree. She earned a PhD in German in 1921 - 45 years after the first African American Dr. Edward Bouchet and 26 years after Dr. W.E.B. DuBois. The years between the two men and the first black woman say a lot about the society that Black women have lived in, endured, and continue to endure and thrive in spite of. Dr. Simpson's spirit and determination during that time speaks volumes to the inner strength of Black women as a people but also highlights times of vulnerability and the imposter syndrome where questions and doubts of skills, competencies, and intellect surface. This chapter is guided by Critical Race Theory's (CRT) tenet - storytelling and counter storytelling - and intersectional theory (IT), where the story of the doctoral journey is told through the lens of a Black woman. My lens, coupled with my experiences, includes the intersectional theoretical concept where aspects of imposter syndrome become paramount - even in 2023. These chapters of my life as a doctoral student and my life after the doctorate will provide the full scope of the successes, challenges, letdowns, and defining moments that constitute the doctoral journey. My goal in writing this chapter is to provide words of encouragement for other Black women who are on or will pursue the same path.

Life Before the Doctorate Degree

I remember the first place in life that truly frightened me was school, specifically 3rd to 5th grade. As a GenXer, the PK-12 space can either love or hate you or both at the same time. Teachers' - whether White, Black or other teachers of color - lacked cultural responsiveness and cultural relevance. Their responses to history were set back almost 200 years. The images in our books were not reflective of my background and teachers lacked effective behavioral management techniques- specifically for Black students. This sent a clear message to me, "You are not welcome here". So, my disgust for school, before my doctorate, started specifically in 3rd to 5th grade. Third grade was a challenge. My teacher always singled me out, picked on me, and fabricated stories about my behavior and academics. As mentioned earlier, the implication was an unsettling feeling of not being welcomed in that setting, so began to drift into a world of television used as an escape from the reality of unwelcomed feeding from a space assumed to be safe. My first therapy session came in the form of animation used to wash away the many tears and fears of the 3rd-grade educational space.

As an outlet, *which was my form of therapy,* I always watched cartoons, especially *Tom and Jerry*. One episode changed my life forever. It was the one episode when I knew I was considered to be different from other people in the world. Not only did I experience this in the PK-12 setting, especially in the 3rd grade, but I also witnessed this through animation. *Tom and Jerry*'s episode called "The Truce Hurts" depicted the mouse, cat, and dog, Butch in blackface. I laughed at this episode up until the image of blackface. I knew then that this was not funny because it mocked my blackness, but being 8 ½ years old in the 3rd grade, I didn't know how to articulate this. Furthermore, as I progressed to 4th grade, things did not get any better. The nature of the teachers' anguish towards me escalated with yelling, screaming, and slamming a textbook on my desk. This would have been a great time for scholars such as Gloria Ladson-Billings, Geneva Gay, and Django Paris to help guide and direct teachers during this time. Their frameworks would propose culturally relevant, responsive, and sustaining pedagogies for students of color but also the frameworks could set the intentionality of trauma-informed practices so that students of color would enjoy the educational space instead of dreading and fearing its many realms of holistic destruction. This is when a traumatic event occurred as I entered the 5th grade.

The PK-12 setting was not a pleasant adventure, but I learned to unwillingly endure it. Though I never stopped feeling as though I stood on a "not welcomed" mat as I entered the classroom, I had so far assumed it would get better as time progressed. As mentioned earlier, teachers' behavior management techniques were ineffective - especially for Black students, so 5th grade was my first encounter with a physical assault on my Black body. My music teacher assumed that I bumped her as other students were pushing and shoving each other in line. I became the focal point of one push right into the music teacher. As a trigger response, she immediately turned around and pulled my Black hair, and threw me against the wall. It was her privileged defense position against a little Black girl who she identified as the aggressor. Although the push was a mistake, my voice again was not heard. Instead, other students of all colors produced a loud guffaw to my traumatic experience and my 5th grade teacher did nothing to soothe my pain. This school setting was not a loving environment as we viewed on television during the 70's and 80's. Not only did the school setting imply that my existence did not matter, but cartoons also reinforced it. I include these examples in my story because it shaped my experiences and my thoughts about education and media combined. If the PK-12 setting did not include images that reflected me in a positive light, if my voice was not heard or were not included in the school curricula, if my favorite cartoon deemed my skin as a curse, and if my Black body did not matter under the physical assault, then where was the lesson? It took me years to find out.

My life before the doctorate degree was at a crossroad both personally and professionally. I graduated high school around the time when Black consciousness, in other words, being "WOKE", was evolving rapidly. The authentic use of "WOKE" expressed itself in various forms from hip-hop music to personal family conscious talks and discussions about society. All in all, the conscious hip-hop music that seized the sound waves through music videos and radio play, was quickly replaced by gangster rap. This was followed by the verdict of the Central Park Five, and the aftermath where teachers, parents, families, and communities failed to inquire about our mental health regarding the five teenagers going to prison for an alleged crime. These examples evoked in me a sense of Kairos (an opportunity to be seized) and Pathos (our response to grief or trauma) because my self-worth and sense of belonging were obsolete in a world that deemed my very existence as criminal.

During this time of identity crisis and confusion, I realized that college right after high school was not in my best interest. Yet I still attended college that fall because of external pressures rather than intrinsic motivation. It was a defining moment to experience the unconditional love of my parents living a dream through me. It all started in 1990, during my first time entering a college building. I started at a community college because my grades and SAT scores were not considered academically acceptable for the 4-year institutions. This lowered my sense of self because I felt like one of the leftovers from a pool of applicants who all tried to reach for more prestigious institutions. Harvard or Yale just wasn't a remote possibility for us. When I was accepted to junior college I was very excited, but also scared. I asked myself, 'what did I sign up for and why'? Of course, my response to myself was to "make my parents and family proud" because I was the first grandchild to go to college. There was an expectation placed so high on me that I couldn't see Mother Earth below anymore. The college setting was another scary environment and an anxious moment.

My anxiety worsened the moment I saw the courses I was given. All my courses were developmental courses because my mathematical computational skills, writing skills and reading comprehension were below basic. Nowadays, whenever I see a course with a zero in front of its title (e.g., 098), my stomach automatically plummets. When in high school, I asked the genie in my imaginary lamp for three wishes: that I would be prepared for the college space, understand how lectures worked, and know how to take notes from verbal presentations. Unfortunately, high school teachers had heavy loads to carry, they were forced to teach through the counter-narrative of the Freirean approach to education, and they had to be therapists to drama disputes. Therefore, I wasn't prepared with those competencies, so I was attending my classes with little understanding of how they worked. For example, I remember one day in a history class, which by the way had a zero in front of the course title, we were told to read the autobiography of *Miss Jane Pittman*. Though the 90s was a time of black consciousness and being "WOKE" my reading skills and comprehension did not match the consciousness of the WOKE scene. I was not prepared for the class discussions in small groups because I never read one chapter of the book. I felt out of place and would question myself - why didn't I want to read the book? Was this the crossroads of reliving the trauma of racism and slavery where Black people are always the conquered and our White counterparts are the victors? Where can I see myself win? Where are the stories about our victories? Will we always be the victims of contempt and pity through text? I thought I was reliving my 3rd to 5th grade nightmare again. I thought maybe I needed to create my own victory but learn the ways of others on how they seemingly became the victors. Even though this sounded nice, it was only for the moment. Since my courses started with zeros, I was not given grades. Instead, students in developmental courses were given P - progress or MP - Making progress. Of course, I earned an MP in all 15 credits of my courses. This meant I had to repeat the courses a 2nd time in the spring semester. Prior to spring, I managed to register for courses which now had a 1 in front of them. This made me feel important - even though I knew that I was not supposed to register for those courses. Since this was a time before online registration, there was no computer to stop me from overriding the system.

Spring started and I attended my courses such as English 101, Math 117, and so forth. I was happy because there were no more courses with zeros to feel like a zero again. This lasted for a good while until the 3rd week of class when the add and drop period started. At this time, our professors were given a finalized list of who was supposed to be in the 100-leveled courses and who was not supposed to be in the 100-leveled courses. I remember this day like it was literally yesterday. My professor of English 101 called me over to the table in the lecture hall and told me "You are not supposed to be in this course. You need to go see your advisor". My professor told me this at the beginning of the class that morning. I had to re-register back to the developmental courses but managed to keep this from my family. I wore a heavy mask throughout the entire semester with my family because I couldn't face the reality of failure as a Black woman. I was devastated.

If my self-esteem and my self-worth were already at a crossroads, the collision of doubt superseded the high expectation above Mother Earth placed on me by my family. I realized that our community places a heavy emphasis on the status of not only being a high school graduate but also a college graduate. This means that you have made history. There were a lot of expectations placed on me not only from my family but also being the oldest of nine grandchildren. As I reflect on these moments, I am reminded that a lot of expectations can work in our favor or be a huge detriment to our mental health and self-esteem. I was a 19-year-old stuck in an alternate reality of continuing my college journey, making sure that my parents loved me regardless, and wearing the mask of a college student who felt out of place. I managed to get through the Spring semester but ended unsuccessfully. Summer semester I made the decision to stop going. This was devastating news to my family. I dropped out and worked full-time as a bank teller. The world of finances, banking, and being around lots of money seemed exciting but frightening. With the ups and downs of customer service, working a robotic 9 to 5 and making little money despite handling so much of it, I decided that this was not the profession for me. I resigned without notice and headed my way back to the same college and picked up exactly where I left off.

I was now a 20-year-old with a new lease on life. I completed my studies at the junior college and went on to a 4-year HBCU to complete the last two years. I earned a Bachelor of Science in English Education, a master's in education, and a master's in public administration. I became a middle-level schoolteacher in the charter school and remained there until I entered a doctoral program. In summary, there were a lot of challenges that I experienced. From feeling unwelcomed at an impressionable age to the moment of contempt and pity through the media assuming that your blackness is indeed a curse to the world, to the pinnacle of realizing that my Black body was devalued and the pain it endured from the physical assault from a teacher was ignored and dismissed. These were defining moments for me because not only did they shape my perception and perspective of the world, but they also shaped the foundation of my skills and competencies for the doctoral journey. Being cognizant that the Black voice was absent in the school curricula, noticing my racial and gendered difference through a cartoon which opened my critical race theory third eye, and experiencing domestic violence in the 5th grade setting from an implied "safe person" challenged me to examine intricate details of an environment. This is what was needed for the doctoral journey. Until the next phase - my life as a doctoral student.

Life as a Doctoral Student

My transition from master-level professional to doctoral level happened in 2010. That year was a difficult time due to the death of my aunt. She was the first in our family to obtain a doctorate degree in education. I admired her for her personal and professional moral obligation to the community, her family, and to herself. In fact, the acknowledgment page of my dissertation is dedicated to her. I applied for several doctoral programs in the city. I was a mother of a young daughter and I had to decide which doctoral program was most feasible within a 5-to-10-mile radius, had scholarship and fellowship opportunities, and with the time I had available to allocate for reading, writing, more reading, and more writing. There were several doctoral programs that I applied to, but only one asked me to come for an interview. During the interview, I felt that I answered the questions efficiently, effectively, and professionally until the committee and department chair of the doctoral program asked, "what is your proposed plan for your research if you are selected?" My response for my research was to explore the overrepresentation of students of color in special education programs. There was no response based on my research idea, but there was a "thank you" and "you will hear from us soon". The following week, I did hear from the committee. It was a rejection letter to the doctoral program. This was a huge disappointment because the program was near my home and the class would meet only once a week. While some argued that a doctoral program was a waste of time, and others flippantly told me a PhD "won't fix your refrigerator" - as if I wanted to do this. Being the brunt of jokes brought me back to the blackface encounter from *Tom and Jerry*. From this experience, I weighed my options again and realized that the doctoral journey does not have to be an in-person experience. I could attend an online university, but I would have to do my best to put aside the stigmas and stereotypes about online instruction for such an advanced and terminal degree.

I was accepted graciously into Capella University where I was able to work at my own pace through an asynchronous modality with intensive modules to complete each week. This doctorate program came equipped with 3-doctoral residencies that had to be completed prior to taking the doctoral comprehensive exams, writing the dissertation proposal, the dissertation, and defense. The coursework was two courses over a 10-week period for spring, summer and fall semesters. I was able to complete the coursework within a year and half and complete the 3-doctoral residencies within the next year. Even though this was not easy, it was well worth it. Taking courses asynchronously where there are deadlines for assignments taught me how to meet deadlines effectively, manage projects, and organize my workload. The importance of attending the doctoral residency was not only the chance of meeting your peers in-person but it also provided the opportunity to participate in panels of PhDs who discussed the comprehensive exams. Hearing the stories and experiences of the exams almost made me drop out of the program but I kept hearing my aunt's voice encouraging me to keep going. Hearing her voice over and over was as real to me as rain on a hot humid summer day. It showed our strength as Black women to reach our many sisters through the spirit world. This is a part of our heritage as people that I am most proud of because her presence during a stressful time of this doctoral program pushed me forward to continue to strive for this accomplishment.

After the 3-doctoral residencies were completed, I had to complete my doctoral comprehensive exams. For the online modality, I was instructed to reach out to the doctoral coordinator and the person who would compile the questions for my exam. The doctoral exam was centered around the proposed research study. At the time, my research topic was too broad, and then it was too narrow where there was little to no literature on that topic that would never publish. Suddenly, there was a mandatory conference call with other doctoral students who completed the coursework and doctoral residencies. We were informed to join the call to discuss possible topics. I finally narrowed it down to exploring through a quantitative methodology teacher morale between two different education contexts. With this new approach, my questions were centered around critical thinking and comparing the strands of qualitative, quantitative, and mixed-methods research to analyze the constructivist approach to teaching and learning. Each response required 16 pages of the doctoral exam for a total of 50 pages. This excluded the reference and title page of the exam. As a doctoral student, I was given 4 weeks to complete and submit to the committee. This was a grueling process to complete. It included late nights and early mornings of working while tending to my eleven-year-old daughter. As a matter of fact, my daughter cooked a lot of meals for dinner while I was stuck buried in printed peer-reviewed journal articles, highlighters, posted notes, and fought with my stubborn printer. Luckily, I had a position with a juvenile facility that allowed me the flexibility of working at home and going to the office. The only regret that I had at the time was not being able to accompany my daughter to certain places and events. Fortunately, she is an understanding person and jumped for joy when I was accepted into the doctoral program.

I grew more confident as completion came closer. I finished the entire exam in the third week in order to give myself another week to read it over. I finally came to the due date of the exam. After I checked the APA in-text citations and reference page, I submitted my paper. There was a sigh of relief and some worry. The protocol for the exam was to pass all three questions. The committee of the institution did not believe in passing a third of the exam or even two-thirds of the exam. It was 3 out of 3 or nothing. Two weeks passed, and I received an email late that evening. The email noted that I did not pass the exam. Two of the three questions did not meet the expectations of the exam committee, but thankfully I was given extensive constructive feedback about where I went wrong. I felt defeated but I was given a 2-week extension to revise the questions. This was great news to me because I had the chance to edit my responses to meet the expectations of the committee. I worked on the questions every day and night. Sometimes I missed meals because I was glued to the work, but I was determined to get this right this time. After all the effort of revising both responses, I resubmitted the doctoral exam. On March 22, 2013, at 6:22 PM, I opened an email that said, *"On behalf of the Dissertation Support Center's School of Education, congratulations on passing your Comprehensive Examination"*. I jumped for joy and immediately told my daughter and then called my parents and sister. They were so excited for me. This was a different feeling from my experiences as a 3rd and 5th grader.

Now I was set for the next phase of this journey - selecting a suitable chair and two committee members for whom I would be writing the dissertation proposal. In some institutions, students are allowed to reach out to different faculty, introduce themselves, and inquire about chair and committee selection. In this case, the online institution generated my topic through a database of faculty to find those whose research interests aligned with mine. As a result, a committee chair, a Black woman, and two committee members were selected for me. I believe that when the stars align, it is for a purpose. I am a Black woman, the first Black woman to earn a PhD was Georgiana Simpson, my committee chair was a Black woman, and my aunt who encouraged me to go for the doctorate was a Black woman. These are the women who helped with this journey. I was quite elated that I had made it this far, but it was unfortunate that my aunt passed in 2010 right around the time I was accepted into the doctoral program. I know that her spirit was with me all the way. I recalled our 3-hour conversations on the phone during my freshman year as a student at the junior college when she said, "You need to go for the Ph.D.". I thought to myself, I just returned to school like a fish out of water who returned to the pond. Can I get used to swimming again before I dive deeper? But her words motivated me to take the chance with confidence.

With my chair and committee members set, I began to write my dissertation proposal. The beginning was not as easy as I assumed. Though I was a great writer, and believed I knew how to construct the lexicon of semantics and syntax to establish a dynamic proposal that I could defend successfully. I was humbled to find out that writing in this stage of your professional academic career is extremely different from master-level writing. I figured that becoming a Doctor of Philosophy of education would be easy because there were no stethoscopes or charts I had to read and no patients I had to see. I was very wrong. One of the analogies that I tell my current doctoral candidates is, "the next time you walk into your doctor's office, ask them 'what was medical school like?' If they tell you it was as easy as making a pie, then quickly leave their office". Earning a doctorate across any discipline is not easy and writing in a doctoral program isn't any easier. The difference between writing at the master-level and writing your dissertation proposal and then dissertation is living on Earth and then traveling to an alternate universe. The writing must jump from a basic foundation to a scholarly-practitioner level. It takes patience, practice, and time, even time away from those you love. In the end it was all worth it.

I started my proposal right after my first meeting with my chair via phone. Between several submissions of my proposal, I went through several iterations which became very frustrating. Finally, it was time for me to defend my dissertation proposal. Capella University set up my defense via conference call on Zoom. After my 30-minute presentation via conference call, my chair and committee had to deliberate while I was put on hold. I put my phone on speaker and walked away while I heard the elevator music playing. I paced back and forth in my home office. Ten minutes went by and I could still hear the music. By this time, my nerves were on edge and the hair stood up on the back of my neck. When they didn't return right away, I thought I had failed yet again. After about thirteen minutes I heard my chair and committee ask "Zakia are you there?" I immediately rushed back to the phone to say, "Yes I'm here". By that time, my chair said, "Zakia, congratulations you have successfully defended your proposal, you have moved from doctoral student to doctoral candidate". Since I was on the phone, I couldn't scream with excitement, but I did clasp my chest to breathe and to make sure that I wasn't dreaming. I felt my aunt's presence all around me that day. At this moment I was Zakia Y. Gates, a doctoral candidate.

I moved on to write the dissertation. I started writing the dissertation in 2014 and completed writing the dissertation at the beginning of 2016. Writing the dissertation was more than just plugging in the pieces from your proposal. This is where you conduct an in-depth analysis and synthesis of the literature, find gaps in the current literature, submit the application to the IRB - Institutional Review Board, obtain approval to conduct your research, collect your data, analyze your results, and discuss your findings. This phase of my journey went through many different iterations. Finally, I was given a defense date of Thursday, December 1, 2016, at 6:00 PM. At the time, I was working as a middle school teacher during the day and teaching as an adjunct faculty at night. On this particular day, my defense was on the same night as my adjunct teaching night which started at 5:30 PM. One thing about completing a dissertation is it is important to let everyone in your immediate family, your friends, and your colleagues know what you are doing. It will give them a better understanding of the journey and it will also lend you a lot of support along the way. My college students, a class of all Black women - again the stars lined up for me - understood the assignment. Black women have and will always see the determination in another Black woman. I remember my sistas saying, "Go ahead Professor, we got you."

The moment came when I had to conduct my dissertation research with a PowerPoint presentation that I sent to my chair and committee a week prior. Again, my defense was via a conference call. I felt more confident this time because I knew my work, the study, justified the research design (causal comparative), justified the methodology (quantitative), explained my findings, described the sample size, explained the statistical tests used, and the measures of central tendency, described my findings and provided recommendations for further research. After my presentation, the committee asked me several questions which I answered thoroughly. They tried to throw me a couple of curve balls, but I knew that this was part of the strategy for a successful defense. By this time it was 7:00 PM, so I was put on hold just like my proposal defense and I heard the elevator music again. Their deliberation took a little longer this time. The chair and committee returned and said, "On behalf of the chair and the committee, we would like to say, congratulations Dr. Zakia Y. Gates you have successfully passed the dissertation defense." I returned to my classroom where my students were working on their research for the course and they asked, "how did it go, professor?". I said, "Oh you can call me doctor". Now I am Dr. Zakia Y. Gates. But what next? What is life after a doctorate degree?

Life After the Doctorate Degree

Life after the doctorate proved to me that success is more than just a terminal degree, it is a lifelong spiritual journey of being in tune with yourself. It is also a way to see how the stars line up or when, as Kendrick Lamar and SZA said, "all the stars are closer". Professionally, life after the doctorate degree made me more marketable in the workforce, I had been a middle school teacher by the time I defended my research, and moving forward I would have more opportunities. It also challenged me to read content outside of my normal comfort zone and provoked me to write at a level that I didn't know existed. Hearing "Dr." as my new professional prefix, at first, was hard to believe. Because my vivid memories and experiences of educational challenges caused me to go through an internal conflict between earning this moment and trying to wake up from a dream.

My life after the doctorate actually became better for me as a Black woman but this also came with some challenges. One of those challenges occurred when I returned to the PK-12 setting after the summer months ended. As I proceeded to decorate my classroom, I noticed that the name on the outside of my classroom was "Ms.". Since I earned my doctorate, I asked the office staff to change the prefix on the front of my classroom door from "Ms." to "Dr." They gladly accommodated me after they congratulated me too. Now my classroom name was Dr. Zakia Y. Gates. The next day our school was holding a night for parents of students to come and visit the classroom of their child's teacher. I heard some parents' voices coming down the hall saying, "Oh wow, so your teacher is a doctor". As they came into the classroom, the father of the student said, "Oh I'm sorry I must be in the wrong room, but I am looking for Dr. Gates". I said sure you are looking at Dr. Gates. The look on his face said it all. He pulled his hand back right away and proceeded to chastise the decorations around my classroom. This was my first experience with the intersectional theory coined by Kimberlee Crenshaw. The father was not used to seeing someone Black with the prefix of doctor, even more so a Black woman.

After going through the motions of my personal and professional obligations of earning a doctorate, and I recalled the concept from Maya Angelou's poetic verse of living the "hope and the dream of the slave" and how that put me in a position of some privilege and challenges. The privilege of earning a doctorate means more professionals take you seriously. You are invited to panel discussions, viewed as a leader, and your work has a footprint. This means professional networks that cover certain themes and topics immediately contact you because it is a part of your research footprint. For instance, I have done extensive research in critical race theory, social justice in education, and extensive literature reviews on the experiences of Black women and Black girls in societal and educational contexts. I have co-authored articles on culturally relevant and responsive pedagogies using the lens of diversity, equity and inclusion. These areas and interests have impacted my professional and personal life after the doctorate. It has also enhanced my leadership competencies in the field of education as a current Assistant Professor. My life after the doctorate enhances my knowledge of content, my knowledge of pedagogy, and my reflection on professional practices. Life after the doctorate establishes a culture for learning and enhances my responsiveness to literature. In addition, publications of my research are uploaded to *Academia Search* and *Research Gate* for other scholars' viewership.

Having the doctorate as a Black woman is a great feat that I accomplished in life. It feels great to be a part of the "2%"

of the population who hold a PhD. This means a lot because being part of the 2% means this journey is not easy. Some colleagues of mine have summoned upon the "PhD blues" concept. I never knew what that meant but there have been times where having the doctorate was too much. Reflecting on this, I had to ask myself, was this the voice of me or the voice(s) of other people? Another educational and personal challenge that occurred during high school. For the first time, I was called a word that I deemed as worse than the historical racial slur constructed for our people. That word was "stupid". This term haunted me for years even after earning the doctorate credential. Being Black and being a woman is a cross cultural conflict against the social constructs that society placed on us. Now being Black, a woman, and a scholar in my work as well as a professor in higher education, brought its own set of challenges too. There is still that stigma that remains among predominantly white institutions (PWIs) where aspects of the imposter syndrome surface many times. The word, "inferior" is used as an explicit way to refer to Black people, in particular Black women, where undermining my intellect has occurred many times in PWIs. Being a Black woman with a PhD, brings questions of my qualifications of being a professor, and leads me to question whether I am able to lead committees through a logical and ethical lens and truly do the work of a professor.

INSPIRATION FOR THE NEXT GENERATION OF DOCTORS

What would I tell the next generation of Doctors to come? Firstly, make sure that you realize you are not alone in your doctoral journey. Since I became a Doctor, I have reached around the World to start sharing the stories of Doctors from all academic disciplines in my show called *The Doc Chat*. As there are over 50+ different types of Doctorate degree majors, individuals need to realize that your doctoral degree journey to becoming a Doctor is very important. It is important not just that you complete your Doctorate degree, but for others around you to see that obtaining a Doctorate degree is possible for them. As a Black male from Indianapolis, Indiana, with a Mother who passed away when I was the age of 13 and a Father who was on and off drugs my entire life, I didn't see myself as having the opportunities laid out for me to be successful in higher education. Even though I had many obstacles to overcome, I did not let them deter me from getting my Doctorate degree. Another valuable lesson I learned on my journey, is that when you start to see doors opening that allow you to obtain a Doctorate degree, don't hesitate to walk right on through. Any fear you might have, does not matter the door is opening for you to obtain a Doctorate degree. It must be for a reason. It took a perfect storm placing me back in my hometown for me to conduct research in an educational area that I was passionate about, and it was a place where I was surrounded by individuals who wanted to support my journey. I remember co-teaching a Doctorate class with the dissertation committee chair who reviewed my defense, and as we were walking out one day he told me, "I know you are going to be one of the ones who is going to finish." The Call even reached my heart at church, as one Sunday morning when I was in the midst of wrapping up some difficult coursework I heard God's voice saying "Dr. John C. Turner, Dr. John C. Turner". All those words echoed in my head as I worked towards my degree for many years, always calling back to mind as things got tough.

Finally, I came to find that not only do you have to believe in yourself but make certain you have people around you who believe in you becoming a Doctor too. I remember being discouraged by several individuals in my life, and they weren't the ones I kept around by the time I finished my Doctoral journey. I remember a young woman who I was dating when I first set out in my Doctorate program who was bothered that I couldn't devote as much time to the relationship as she wanted. It was painful to hear her say, "your Doctorate degree really isn't that important, John." When I heard that, the relationship had to end. The real ones in your life will help you get to the finish line. They may not understand everything that you are doing, but they will know how important completing your Doctorate degree is for you and your future. Continue to seek revelation and guidance from Jesus Christ above all, and next the ones who care about your success. Talk to your mentors, other Doctors, or people who will lift you up when you feel down or alone. A mere 2% of the entire world's population are recognized as Doctors, and the world needs you to become the next one.

– DR. JOHN C. TURNER

So you want to become a DOCTOR? Let me share some things no one is telling you about becoming a Doctor… (Post from LinkedIN 2023 by Dr. John C. Turner)

1. Not everyone is going to call you "Doctor" every time they see you when you complete your degree. You must learn to be ok with that & swallow your pride. No one is going to take your Doctorate degree away if you're not called Doctor by everyone who you run into. It may not happen depending on your professional setting as well, so you must be prepared for that.

2. There are ALL KINDS of Doctorate degrees out there. From Ph.D., Ed.D., M.D., D.O., J.D., DNP, DMin., and on and on. Some Doctors complete dissertations, while others complete projects. All important to note when you meet Doctors & learn about their completion of their Doctoral programs. Research different Doctoral programs & see what degree route will be right for you to pursue & your future, as this will save you a lot of time, money, & mental/physical/emotional stress.

3. Three bars on the arms of a graduation robe are a constant reminder that a Doctorate degree has been completed. Depending on the completed Doctorate degree institution, the hood color, robe, tassel, & tam will be different & represent that Doctorate degree distinction & institution.

4. Not everyone who enters a Doctorate degree program finish. The statistics show about 50% of individuals complete these degrees. "Doctoral Candidate", "ABD" (All But Dissertation), & "Doctoral Student" in name titles means these individuals are possibly working towards completing a Doctorate degree, but they are not done and have not become Doctors yet.

5. It is important to know what you want to research, know what faculty you want to conduct research with, & know who is going to pay for you to do this research if you want to complete a Doctorate degree. There are great gaps in research that need to be done by Doctorate students & people who will fully fund your Doctorate degree for you to do it for FREE!

6. When you complete a Doctorate degree, it does not automatically mean the job world is going to open wide up for you. You still must put in the work, continue to research & write, plus carve out a niche in your profession to become well known in a passion area of work you have for yourself.

7. Your title of "Dr." only needs to be referenced once in your name. It's either "Dr. Name" or "Name, Ph.D.". Go with which one works best for you. A Doctor's credentials don't have to be referenced twice in one's name.

8. You do not have to get a Doctorate degree & only become a Professor in that field. Doctorate degree holders are CEOs, Speakers, Entrepreneurs, Non-Profit Leaders, Authors, & work in many careers.

9. If you are unsure how to navigate becoming a Doctor, PLEASE ASK! Many of us never in our wildest dreams ever saw ourselves becoming Doctors! Asking questions on how to become a Doctor from Doctors will help you reach your Doctorate degree dreams!

INSPIRATION FOR THE NEXT GENERATION OF DOCTORS

Pursuing a doctorate degree is an individual journey that can be daunting yet rewarding. One must know themselves or be willing to get there. You must find what motivates you to persevere through life's inevitable peaks and valleys. No matter what it is you chase in life, whether it be a graduate degree, a new business venture, changing careers, or expanding a family, it is important to be grateful and reflect on the lessons learned as you grow along the way. For healthcare leaders, it is imperative that we educate ourselves and holistically evaluate global healthcare systems to find solutions that improve patient's quality of life and the healthcare system overall. A doctorate degree is a major step towards addressing unmet medical needs and fighting injustice. To do so we need to become advocates who are equipped with the proper knowledge and tools. For as long as I can remember I have been influenced by strong leaders to make a difference in someone else's life. I now have that opportunity and responsibility and I carry it with pride and honor.

– DR. ANTHONY K. TAYLOR

INSPIRATION FOR THE NEXT GENERATION OF DOCTORS

In my narrative teaches anything or offers anyone in the struggle or considering the struggle, because getting a doctorate degree is definitely a struggle, anything, let it be this. The journey is yours and yours alone. It might imitate another's, but it can never duplicate another, and your story will never be replicated. Therefore, you must do what works best for you (and your family). But is that all, Dr. Randolph? Of course not. If authenticity were the sole key to attainment, everyone could, and most would. Nevertheless, statistics and research show that a very small percentage of the world attains this level. Thus, I present some of my impartation of wisdom, advice, and lessons I learned below.

Remember your why! I tell students this all the time. If you are unaware, disconnected, and fail to comprehend why you are enduring what sometimes may feel like unending and unconquerable drudgery, there is no basis for motivation or inspiration, internally or externally.

There are many people who will begin the race or, better yet, the journey to becoming a doctor with you but will be absent or silent upon completion. Some may even appear happy for you. However, life has a way of shaking people loose, and everyone who starts the race with you will not meet you at the finish line. The allegory is not only implicit to students who began a program the same semester or cohort as you. It is also indicative of those in your life outside of the metaphorical classroom. Not everyone will support or clap for you, which is perfectly acceptable if you remember your why. If said persons are not composite to your why, they are inconsequential.

Perfection is not possible, and neither should it be the goal. I literally drove myself partly insane or perhaps drove myself completely insane attempting to accomplish this feat. There is no credible or accredited school on this earth comprised where 100% of professors who will give any student 100% of the possible points 100% of the time. One professor told me they don't even start grading at 100%. So, save your brain cells and your blood pressure reading. At the first residency, another professor from my university told us that B's make degrees. While my personal ascription was not to such a thought paradigm, it is true. Conclusively, the diploma says "Doctor," not "Doctor with a 4.0." If perfection isn't met, the world will not end, and the earth will not stop rotating on its axis.

If not perfection, then what? Strive for excellence, exceptional, extraordinary, exhilarating, and enlightening. The goal of the journey and the degree is to add meaningful and even innovative contributions to the existing body of knowledge regarding your subject matter. It isn't perfection; therefore, it's better to operate in exceeding eminence in your quest to become an expert in your field.

Find some form of a support group, even if that is just you and one or two other people. It can be peers, social media groups, or others you know who already have a doctorate. Having someone who "gets it" is crucial. The above gems of advice are by no means an exhaustive list. There exists a plethora of wisdom and knowledge I have learned and not told here, but that could be told if word limitations did not constrain me. Some advice is interwoven in earlier sections of this chapter and throughout this manuscript from each vantage point. Use it as a beacon to guide you if you are embarking on or seeking to embark upon the journey. By this juncture, the thought may have entered your mind that perhaps this doctoral road can be lonely. It can be and at times it is. For instance, when you are the only person awake in your house at 1:00 or 2:00 a.m. studying, reading, writing, or researching if you live alone and are awake at that hour at your computer, it can leave you feeling like you are the only soul on earth, human or otherwise, who is awake, cognizant, and doing work. There is so much more of my journey I want to share and perhaps one day I will. Most people do not understand unless they have achieved at this level, and even some of them still won't appreciate your pursuit of excellence in academic rigor. Nevertheless, hold fast to the desire to achieve and never falter in the belief that you can reach the finish line. Remember, run your race and no one else's.

– Dr. KHANDICIA RANDOLPH

INSPIRATION FOR THE NEXT GENERATION OF DOCTORS

Go after your dreams. Do not allow anyone to discourage you from being the best you that you can be. Go straight to college from high school. Take full advantage of the opportunity to grow and learn in a safe environment. Explore yourself and the world before you become a parent or a spouse. It is hard to raise a little person while you are still a kid yourself. This is the time to move wherever you want and do whatever you want. Once you become responsible for other people, it becomes more difficult to do certain things. But difficult does not equate impossible. If you do have a family before you reach your goals, don't fret, you can still reach your goals. However, you should consider your family unit when you make decisions. While a decision might be the best decision for your family, it may not be the best decision for you personally or professionally. Don't settle when choosing a partner. Look for someone who will love, cherish, support, and care for you unconditionally. Pursuing a doctorate is a long, hard, and ultimately rewarding experience. Be prepared to lose people along the way, whether you need to cut them out for holding you back or they walk away because of your pursuit. Some people will be happy for you and your accomplishments.

Many others will not. Don't be surprised when some people refuse to call you doctor. You will be a doctor despite it all! Once you have decided that you want to pursue a doctoral degree, do your research to find the best institution for your needs. Look at the admission requirements and the program curriculum to ensure that it is in line with your qualifications and goals. Review the cost and payment structure. It is easy to end up in massive debt pursuing higher education. There are many scholarships available to help people achieve their higher education goals.

You do not want to add any unnecessary financial burden on top of what will already be a challenging journey. Consider your professional situation and how a doctoral program could impact your career. Learn everything you can from those who have already been in your position, and where you are headed. When your boss asks you to do something extra, see it as a learning opportunity rather than just extra work. Those additional assignments can lead to valuable experience or a promotion if you prove you are dependable and skilled. Pay attention when professionals talk. You will be surprised at the wisdom you will glean from actively listening. Take additional professional classes, courses, and certifications. Invest, invest, and invest some more. You should invest in yourself professionally and personally. Invest in real estate and the stock market. Take full advantage of your company's 401k or 403b program. Don't stop until you have achieved the highest level of education you want or need to get, keep, and advance in your chosen career field. Don't give up. You've got this. We want you to stand on our shoulders. We are here cheering you on and reaching back to help you up. I plan to use my platform to help and encourage others to achieve their educational and professional goals. I am my sister's and brother's keeper.

– DR. SAMARIA R. ROBERTS-WASHINGTON

INSPIRATION FOR THE NEXT GENERATION OF DOCTORS

As I think about these tips for the next generation of Doctors that we're going to see and need in our world, these are some suggestions that I will leave for them to be successful in their journey:

Don't spend all the time thinking you have to get the work done today, you must take some time to breathe. It will feel like and be a suffocating process at times. If you're stressed out and laid out, how will you get done? Take a walk, exercise, back up, and then come back to it. Mental health and physical health are important when you are doing this work.

Know that having the right people involved in your process is very important as well. People come and go, but make sure not only you have the right people around you in your program, but also the right people around you outside of your program. Have those inspiring people that want to see you win, help you win, and want to see you finish. The Professors want to see you win because it looks good for you and good for them too. We need a culture of care when we're dealing with students because it's a lot to take on. You are going to do some amazing work, but it's going to take some time. Make sure you realize that your time and having the right people around you is important so that you can truly get to that finish line and complete your doctorate degree. Our world needs you as a Doctor and know that you can make it, trust me, you really can.

– DR. TRENTON WATSON

INSPIRATION FOR THE NEXT GENERATION OF DOCTORS

As a Black woman, I am the second in my family to earn a PhD but not the first Black woman overall. I encourage Black women to always strive to complete the doctoral journey. If you are a Black woman currently in a doctoral program, please make sure to find and attach yourself to other Black women on the same journey. Find doctoral support groups. This is especially helpful when writing the dissertation. Writing the dissertation can be a lonely time but starting dissertation writing clubs, just as there are book clubs, will help build a community of learners and a community of future Black women scholars.

– DR. ZAKIA GATES

The Doctor Talker

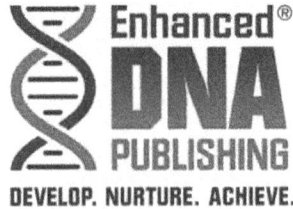

www.ingramcontent.com/pod-product-compliance
Lightning Source LLC
Chambersburg PA
CBHW051944160426
43198CB00013B/2290